Parental drug misuse – a review of impact and intervention studies

by Jo Tunnard

research in practice

w w w . r i p . o r g . u k

This pamphlet is provided free of charge to our Partners and
Members and is also available to them in full on the Partners' and
Members' pages of our website www.rip.org.uk. Others may
purchase copies (£5 including p&p) through our website or our
Dartington office. This series is an example of a wider range of
activities that together support the adoption and implementation of
research findings. More information about **research** in **practice** can
be found on the cover and on the website.

Published 2002
ISBN 0-9542562-0-4

Other titles in the series:
The Education of Children in Need: a research overview
Ruth Sinclair, 1998
ISBN 0-9541834-3-6

Children and Domestic Violence: a research overview of the impact on children
Catherine Humphreys and Audrey Mullender, 2000
ISBN 0-9541834-2-8

Commissioning and managing external research: a guide for child care agencies
edited by Jo Tunnard, 2001
ISBN 0-9541834-1-X

Parental problem drinking and its impact on children
Jo Tunnard, 2002
ISBN 0-9541834-0-1

about this pamphlet

One of the main ambitions of **research in practice** is to make it easier for local authorities and voluntary organisations to access reliable research, distilled and translated with a particular audience in mind. This series of occasional pamphlets covers key practice areas, identified by practitioners, and key research strategy issues, identified by planners and policy makers. The work and methods of **research in practice** chime well with the developing national agenda to build more effective, comparable services for children, in part by creating and using reliable research evidence.

The topic for this research review emerged from discussions with practitioners and their managers over a number of years. While there is often a good deal of research information available on the impact on the person with a particular problem – as there is indeed in the case of drug use – there is often little on the impact of the problem on those who live close to the problem. And yet this is the very area in which social care workers are charged with making life-changing assessments.

Much of what is written on the subject of this pamphlet is covered under the title of substance misuse, where potential problems and services discussed relate to both drugs and alcohol. Social care workers tell us how important it is for them to get information about drugs or alcohol – there are many similarities but more differences. As a response to these concerns we have commissioned two, linked, reviews of impact on children – this one on parental drug misuse, a 'sister' to the publication earlier this year on parental problem drinking.

As with the previous pamphlet, this one has been peer reviewed by a range of academics based in both universities and service agencies, practitioners and those seeking to assist the development of evidence based practice. We are grateful to them all for their generosity of time and good advice – what follows here has benefited enormously from their wisdom: Christine Ballinger, Leandra Box, Liz Brown, Barry Crossley, Jonathen Eckersley, Viv Evans, Donald Forrester, Di Hart, Peter Harwood, Judith Harwin, Carol Hayden, Zarrina Kurtz, Neil McKeganey, Hugh McLaughlin, Michael Matkin, Peter Nash, Tony Newman, Jim Orford, Jane Powell, Chris Rainey, John Randall, Mary Ryan, Theresa Salter, Simon Thompson, Pam Watson, John Wilkinson and John Woolham. Special thanks to DrugScope, for their excellent library and cataloguing system, and to Michael Murphy and Sandra Jerrim for their generous advice and support in addition to their peer review.

Celia Atherton
Director of **research in practice**

contents

introduction

summary of findings and contents

- The use of drugs can have an adverse impact, not just on the health and behaviour of parents, but on the lives of children too. This 'drug misuse' or 'problem drug use' is the focus of this review. The findings do not relate to all parents who use drugs, as many provide their children with warmth and stability. It is important to look at people's behaviour, not the label that may have been applied to them.
- The impact on children can affect all areas of their life – home, school and community.
  There are more UK and Irish studies about drugs than about alcohol but the numbers affected by drugs are smaller. One million children are estimated to be living in families with problem drinking – probably at least four times greater than the number affected by problem drug use.
- This discrepancy in research material reflects, in part, the greater interest at government level in dealing with drug-related problems, and in matching that interest with cash investments and policy initiatives.
- Studies point to the key role for practitioners in helping children and familes. The messages are about both the content and style of service delivery. Effort needs to be targeted at reducing the risk factors and boosting the protective factors in children's lives. Parents value local, accessible and child-friendly services where adult and child concerns can be dealt with at the same time and where individuals feel welcomed and not judged badly.

This review examines the available research about both the impact of problem drug use and interventions designed to reduce that impact. It starts by looking at definitions, the extent of problem drug use, and its impact across important aspects of children's lives. These are linked to the dimensions that practitioners will be familiar with through their use of the Assessment Framework for Children in Need (C1)*. Messages for practice are then drawn from both the impact and intervention studies. The studies are those already published in the UK and Ireland, and conducted over the past ten years or so. Some intervention studies from the USA have been included because of the lack of such material in UK and Irish research.

The review is intended for social care workers involved with adults – using or affected by drugs – and their children and young relatives. Beyond social services, it is intended for probation workers, health visitors and midwives, teachers and those delivering drug services. Beyond front-line staff and their managers, it is intended for use by Primary Care Trust commissioners and others planning or conducting service reviews, in single or multi-agency work.

* For an explanation of this referencing system, see p11 (how the review was organised)

the focus on drugs other than alcohol

An earlier review in this series has focused on parental problem drinking and its impact on children (C2). Many studies consider the two problems together and there is an argument for doing so, given that the difficulties that arise in households are similar in some respects, and given that many parents use a combination of both sorts of drug.

But there are important differences too. Drug use is usually a private activity, in part at least because some drugs are illegal. The secrecy and the stigma that attach to the lifestyle of some users can impose a particularly severe constraint on those close to them. Lack of money is more likely to be a worry, as is the fear of possible arrest and imprisonment if income has to be supplemented from other sources such as theft, fraud, sex work and drug dealing. And within the home there are the hazards – overall more serious than with alcohol – from the drugs themselves, from equipment, and from the risk of infectious diseases.

For these reasons it seems important to focus on problem drug use separately, whilst recognising that an understanding of both alcohol and other drugs – and of the research evidence available – will be needed for both practice and policy work. Where reference is made to studies that include alcohol, an attempt has been made to include only the findings that relate to drugs.

defining 'parental drug misuse'

Many parents who use drugs will be maintaining a caring and organised household – the fact that a parent is using drugs does not necessarily equate with deficits in parenting capacity. For the purpose of this review we are concerned with drug use by parents which professionals or family members consider is having an adverse impact, not just on the health and behaviour of parents, but on the lives of their children also. We refer to this in the text as either 'drug misuse' or 'problem drug use'.

Many children have adults other than parents as primary carers, perhaps more so in the case of the children in this particular review. Generally, for the sake of brevity, we use the word 'parent' to include these other adults. But where research studies are making a point about particular adults – such as grandparents or partners in reconstituted families – we use those specific terms.

the size of the problem

There is consensus among researchers and other commentators that it is difficult to get clear figures about the scale of parental problem drug use and the number of children affected. There are various reasons for this gap in knowledge. One is the lack of specific data about parents – rather than persons – who use drugs. Another is the lack of information about the number of parents who misuse drugs but are not in touch with services and – conversely – the number of drug-using parents in touch with services for reasons unconnected with their drug use. An additional difficulty in gauging the size of the problem arises because drugs and alcohol are usually considered together, especially in social services recording systems, making it difficult to tease out the data relating to one rather than the other.

Nevertheless, several assertions can be made with some certainty:

- An estimated 266,000 adults have problematic drug use in Great Britain.
- At a national level, the profile of people who use drugs is changing. There are more women than previously; they are younger; many who are parents are children themselves; there is a wider range of drugs being used; and a greater degree of polydrug use (where drugs – including alcohol – are taken in combination).
- Heroin (and alcohol) are the main causes of concern, as measured by people seeking and getting treatment, but with significant recent increases in the use of cocaine. The majority of heroin users are of childbearing age and many of them have children.
- Considerable numbers of women who either get in touch with drug treatment centres or then go on to use those services have dependent children.

For more detailed information about the national picture see C3-C6.

Local information can usually help flesh out the national picture. But there are difficulties here, too, in trying to determine prevalence. An important one is the over reliance on data about child protection registrations and care proceedings. Whilst these figures tell us something about current professional practice and the operation of thresholds by the court and other agencies, they are – on their own – necessarily limited in what they tell us about whether the thresholds are right in terms of addressing the needs arising from the impact on children of parental drug misuse.

What we can say from local audits of need is the following:

- Children and parents with needs arising from parental substance misuse (alcohol or drugs or both) emerge as a discrete cluster in most localities.
- There are variations in the size of this group, but recent audits indicate that parental drug misuse is a factor in up to 15 per cent of open caseloads and in up to 20 per cent of children newly looked after.
- Families have often not been in contact with social services until their situation has deteriorated to the point of family breakdown or significant risk for the children.
- The services offered tend to focus on protecting children from

the worst consequences of parental drug use rather than helping parents change their use of drugs. While many children stay at home or return home, to the care of parents or other relatives, new crises often result in new interventions.

- Parental mental health difficulties feature highly.

For more information about local audits see C7.

the policy context

The last three decades have seen considerable shifts in thinking and action about drug use. The prevailing view in the 1970s was that drug use was an illness, requiring long-term medication, and with help provided exclusively via the health service. The emphasis changed in the 1980s, with rising concern about AIDS and HIV. The health hazards led to programmes of risk reduction, with direct help to users in the form of needle exchanges and the promotion of prescribed drugs to reduce injecting. The current focus is directed more to the criminal and other anti-social behaviour that can attach to the use of drugs. Attempts to change behaviour have come to the forefront of political thinking, fuelling programmes to reduce dependency and address the reasons behind drug use. There has also been renewed debate about the relative value of relaxing penalties for the possession of drugs, strengthening sanctions against dealers and traffickers, and shifting resources into treatment.

The Government's ten-year National Strategy for tackling drugs aims to reduce the availability of illegal drugs on the streets, help young people resist using drugs, protect communities and increase access to treatment and rehabilitation (C8). It has little to say about parental drug misuse, bar a fleeting reference to the importance of assessing the needs of children and providing services to safeguard their welfare. In response, the Scottish Executive has been pro-active in helping local Drug Action Teams and Area Child Protection Committees develop joint policies, procedures, practice and training to underpin work with children and their families (C3).

Recent initiatives have increased the availability of services. All areas have some sort of health provision – for detoxification treatment and the prescribing of substitute drugs – and most also have some degree of community-based service. Nevertheless, services remain patchy and inconsistent and in some areas they do not include attention to alcohol misuse. The lack of a national strategy on alcohol is blamed for this widening gap between alcohol and drug services.

The last decade has seen, too, an increase in spending on research and evaluation. One 'of the most ambitious projects, the National Treatment Outcome Research Study (NTORS) is the largest treatment follow up in the UK (C9). It has been tracking over 1,000 drug agency clients since 1995 with a view to learning about the long-term outcomes of programmes providing methadone maintenance, methadone reduction, residential rehabilitation and specialist in-patient treatment. Smaller studies include the impact of waiting times, the needs and services for people with both substance misuse and mental health problems, and evidence about the psychosocial consequences of drug misuse.

how this review was organised

The research review set out to collect and analyse material that social care professionals would find helpful. The preparatory work high-lighted the rather complex nature of the work. Computer database searches in child care, drug and medical organisations – using key words – each produced several hundred international research and practice references for the past five years alone. What was heartening, though, was the discovery of more UK and Irish research studies (albeit small in scale) than had been anticipated as a result of preparing the earlier review, of parental problem drinking (C2).

This review focuses on relevant research studies conducted in the UK and Ireland during the past ten or so years. Besides setting a boundary for the work, this decision was influenced by the view that any earlier studies would probably be less relevant to the current use of drugs.

Another dilemma relates to the international studies referenced in the UK and Irish studies and other material. The review wanted to avoid the tendency of saying that studies conducted elsewhere may not be generalisable to the home situation but then failing to indicate which are, which are not, and why. Such a detailed analysis was beyond the remit of the review. Nevertheless, studies from other countries are of some interest, and on this topic no less than others. As a result, the review includes information from international studies but presents it separately from the UK and Irish data.

The international studies, mainly from the USA, are not referenced individually, although most were read whilst preparing this review. Instead, the 'lessons from other countries' sections of this review draw heavily on the work of Diane Hogan (A1) as her comprehensive literature review of the international data analyses the studies succinctly and removes the need to repeat that work. Her work has the added advantage, for this review, of also focusing exclusively on drugs other than alcohol.

Several other reviews that include a mix of UK and international studies are referenced (A2-A4) because their particular focus will be of interest to some readers.

The next question was about how to analyse and present the research data. Twenty-two studies are included – 13 explore the impact of problem drug use whilst the other nine report on interventions to reduce its impact on children and families. Inevitably, there is some overlap between the two groups because the impact studies also throw light on what can be done to help families and the intervention studies tell us something about the needs that services are intended to address.

Readers will want to know whether the studies are all equally important. Various criteria could be applied here. One is sample size – and several of the studies are very small indeed. Another is the source of information – evidence from just one source, or from case work files, is necessarily limited. For this review, two criteria have been judged particularly important.

The first is whether the studies include control groups - this means that one group of children get the service being tested whilst a similar, matched group of children get a different service. As a result, the findings are more likely to relate to what is being studied rather than to any other influences at work. The second criterion is whether the studies help us understand the factors that might make a difference to children's outcomes. This is about looking beyond statistics about service outputs – such as child protection registration, care orders, placement decisions – and examining both family experiences and outcomes. Outputs are relatively easy to measure, but they are rather poor at helping us understand what can be done to promote positive change in children's health and development and quality of life.

The chart on page 47 summarises the twenty two studies and also highlights these two criteria - the use of control groups and the focus on family perspectives and outcomes. The studies cluster in the following way:

impact studies, with control group – 4 studies

impact studies, no control group – 9 studies

intervention studies, with control group – 2 studies

intervention studies, no control group – 7 studies.

References and other materials relied on have been organised as follows at the end of the review:

A   research and literature reviews

B   the 22 studies reviewed

C   practice and policy documents.

A final list sets out the references alphabetically by author.

what drugs do to you

This section highlights some of the key characteristics of certain drugs. It is intended to help readers who are not familiar with drugs' work to understand better both the impact of the drugs on family members and the research material included in the review.

Some commentators describe drugs as clustering into three main groups:

downers – mainly opiates (drugs derived from the opium poppy) such as heroin, methadone, morphine and codeine, but also alcohol and some medication prescribed for anxiety and depression. These can be used recreationally but they carry a risk of physical and psychological dependence.

uppers – mainly cocaine, crack cocaine and amphetamine. They, too, can be used recreationally but there is a risk of psychological dependence and of severe downside reactions.

sideways movers – mainly cannabis, LSD, ecstasy and mushrooms. They leave the body as it is but change our perceptions.

The focus of this section – like the studies reviewed – is on downers and uppers rather than the sideways movers.

Although the drugs are described separately, it is important to note that drugs are often used in combination – this is called polydrug use. If two stimulants or two depressants are taken together, they are likely to have an additive effect, thus increasing the stimulation or depression. Mixing different sorts of drugs is likely to have more unpredictable consequences.

More detailed information about particular drugs can be found in C10 and C11.

HEROIN

Heroin is made from the opium poppy and reduces pain and anxiety when absorbed into the bloodstream. It is the most powerful known painkiller, and is usually injected or smoked rather than sniffed. Its advantage over other opiates is that it takes effect relatively quickly and – apart from initial discomfort in first-time users – has relatively few undesirable side effects. The advantage of injecting is that the impact is more immediate and stronger because none of the drug is lost before entering the bloodstream.

Heroin produces a feeling of warmth and drowsy contentment that helps cushion the user from the psychological impact of pain, fear and anxiety. The worries are still felt but they seem to matter less, and the user can continue to think, talk and act coherently. It is only at higher doses that sedation takes over and the user becomes drowsy.

A disadvantage is that tolerance to heroin develops quickly so there's a need to increase the amount taken – or change the way it is taken – to continue to feel the full effect. Dependence also develops quickly, so there is a need to keep taking the drug just to feel 'normal'. Suddenly stopping taking heroin can produce severe nausea, vomiting, cramps, aches and sleeplessness. These symptoms last for over a week and can be followed by both lethargy and craving for the drug for several months. Stopping and starting can lead to loss of tolerance and the risk that the user will overdose if the normal dose is returned to after a break.

In women, a major side effect of heavy and regular use is the loss of menstrual periods. But heroin ceases to be the contraceptive it is often thought to be if the level of intake is reduced. As a result, women may be surprised to find they are pregnant.

Heroin withdrawal during pregnancy can result in foetal distress, so stable doses or controlled reduction is required rather than the mother ceasing her use completely before the birth. Continued use during pregnancy slows down the development of the foetus and, as a result, is associated with low birth weight and premature delivery. After birth babies may suffer severe withdrawal symptoms because the heroin in the mother's bloodstream is no longer available.

Treatment is mainly by methadone (see below). A few doctors are licensed to prescribe heroin but most do not do so because of the cost of both the drug itself and the long-term need for support services for users.

METHADONE

Methadone is a synthetic opiate that, unlike heroin, works well when swallowed, and is usually taken in liquid form. It is taken as a substitute for heroin and used in treatment programmes to help heroin users reduce their drug intake in a controlled way and to avoid the problems associated with injecting heroin. Methadone cannot be injected. It has similar, but less intense, effects than heroin. It tends to be longer acting and it can be taken once a day by someone who is dependent without them experiencing withdrawal symptoms. As with heroin, users who have a stable and hygienic lifestyle can be indistinguishable from non-drug users and can remain free of serious physical damage. Some users value methadone because it enables them to feel well and regain stability, but many are reluctant to use it because of its negative aspects – it rots the teeth, produces intense aching in the bones, stays in the body longer than heroin, and is much harder to 'come off'.

In new babies of methadone-using mothers the withdrawal symptoms may be more severe than for heroin. They also tend to start later, several days after birth, and this can cause consternation and disappointment to mothers who may have expected that their own control of heroin would have had a positive impact on their baby.

Treatment aims to enable the user to become drug free (detox-ification or reduction programme) by using methadone to gradually eliminate the withdrawal symptoms from stopping heroin intake, or to stabilise intake (maintenance programme) whilst at the same time reducing harm from injecting or having to buy heroin.

SUBUTEX

This is another synthetic opiate prescribed as an alternative to heroin. It is becoming increasingly popular at present, in part because of its advantages over methadone – it is less toxic and so less problematic if taken accidentally. It also acts as a blocker to the effects of heroin and so reduces the need for people to 'top up' their subutex dose with heroin.

COCAINE

Cocaine is derived from the leaves of the coca shrub. It is a white powder, generally sniffed up the nose in small quantities through a tube and absorbed into the bloodstream through the nasal membranes. It can also be smoked or injected.

It is a powerful stimulant, producing almost immediate but short-lived feelings of enhanced alertness, energy and confidence. The euphoria is such that users want to repeat the experience, thus leading to psychological dependence on the pleasurable effects. Regular use tends to result in feelings of nausea, restlessness, insomnia and weight loss. At the extreme end users may be excitable, highly nervous, exhausted and with a state of mind similar to paranoid psychosis. But, unlike heroin, cocaine use is not marked by tolerance or withdrawal symptoms. The effects generally clear up when use stops, though feelings of tiredness and depression may persist (and the user knows that these will reduce quickly if more cocaine is taken).

If taken during pregnancy, cocaine decreases foetal blood flow and is associated with congenital abnormalities that affect the genito-urinary tract and the heart, limbs and face. Like heroin, there is an association with low birth weight and reduced body length.

Treatment is difficult because there is no effective substitute drug to encourage users into treatment. Tranquillisers or anti-depressants may help.

CRACK COCAINE

This is cocaine that has been treated with chemicals to allow the drug to be smoked more easily and absorbed more quickly. It comes in the form of small nuggets the size of raisins. The effects are similar to cocaine, but more immediate, intense and short lived. Use can cause chest pains and breathing problems. The treatment difficulties are as for cocaine, above.

AMPHETAMINE

Amphetamine is a synthetic stimulant produced in powder, tablet or paste form. It is generally sniffed up the nose or injected but it can also be smoked, or dabbed onto the tongue, or dissolved in drinks. It stimulates the nervous system so the effect is similar to when adrenaline rushes through the body at times of stress.

Like cocaine, the drug produces feelings of intense exhilaration and heightened physical and mental capacity. But it has side effects – mood swings, acute anxiety, irritability and restlessness. The effects take longer than cocaine to wear off – users can be left feeling tired and low for a couple of days.

Regular users can become run down because of lack of food and sleep, and heavy users can experience severe depression. Increasing the dose can provide toxic effects such as delusion, hallucinations and feelings of paranoia, sometimes leading to hostility against imagined attacks. Increased irritability, aggression and impaired judgement are the most worrying side effects.

For babies of amphetamine-using mothers during pregnancy, there are concerns about growth retardation and premature delivery. And, as with heroin and methadone, there are withdrawal symptoms that include abnormal sleep patterns, poor feeding, body tremors and muscle rigidity. These symptoms tend to disappear, but may take several months to do so. Treatment difficulties are as for cocaine, above.

the impact on the lives of children and families

In this section we explore what the research studies tell us about the main dimensions of children's lives – their living situation, their family and social relationships, and their behaviour, health and education. Sub-headings are linked to the Assessment Framework for Children in Need (C1), with reference to either one of the three domains (child's developmental needs, parenting capacity, family and environmental factors) or one of the twenty dimensions attached to the domains. Issues of child protection are incorporated into the main body of the text rather than being treated in a separate section. This reflects the approach to practice that underpins the Assessment Framework – child protection and need are best not seen as two separate areas of work. The starting point is to identify what is needed, and sometimes this will include protection (C36). The focus is on findings from UK and Irish studies, with an end note summarising findings from USA (and occasionally other) studies.

summary

living situation

- Poor living conditions are seen as both a cause and effect of parental drug use. The strain of finding money for drugs can add to family tensions and leave parents unavailable for their children.
- Parents have a strong awareness of their child care responsibilities but may struggle to provide stable routines and a safe home.
- Some degree of neglect is highly likely where household resources, both financial and emotional, are invested in the pursuit and use of drugs.

family & social relationships

- Babies born with drug withdrawal symptoms are very difficult to care for, and this may act as a block to early bonding.
- Separations are common, because of parents being in residential treatment or custody, or because children are placed away from home, sometimes separate from their siblings.
- Relationships between parents vary. Some mothers found their partners supportive, others were troubled by conflict and isolation.
- Grandparents are often a positive influence and can provide considerable support.
- Children can feel upset and isolated, sometimes because of extra responsibilities at home.

behaviour

- A high proportion of parents have been involved in the criminal justice system.
- Parents use a range of strategies for protecting children from

disputes about drugs and from the consequences of their drug use.

- Parents fear that children might copy their drug use, either seeing it as normal behaviour or in order to escape from difficulties and deprivation.
- Pregnancy acts as a strong incentive to women to make a break with the past. Starting a methadone treatment programme is another protective factor.

health

- Children's health is put at risk through foetal exposure to drugs, but the longer-term outcome is encouraging.
- Children's confidence and self-esteem can be dented by their parents' unpredictable behaviour, and by the rejection of peers.
- Many parents have mental health problems, especially depression. Using drugs is often a way of coping with stressful events or life circumstances.

education

- Children's play and leisure opportunities may be affected by parental drug use.
- Starting school may expose the problems that children and parents have been facing.
- Parents are fearful that their children will be isolated, teased or bullied at school for the parents' lifestyle.
- School can help motivate both parents and children.

the impact on living situation

All the UK studies were conducted in inner-city areas marked by poverty and other deprivation so, inevitably, these factors predominate in descriptions of those who make up the sample. Poor living conditions are seen as both a cause and effect of parental drug use (B11), but the stresses associated with drug use are additional to those arising from socio-economic circumstances (B4).

housing (Assessment Framework [AF] - family & environmental factors)

Families tended to be living in below standard housing. In one study a quarter of the parents had no home of their own and were living with relatives or friends, whilst another third were in temporary housing, including bed and breakfast hotels (B5). Other parents were more settled, but suffered from living in areas characterised by high levels of crime, drug dealing and drug use (B8, B11).

income [AF - family & environmental factors]

With few parents in any study in paid work, and families mainly dependent on welfare benefits, income levels were very low. Three-quarters of the families in one study reported having a total income of less than £300 per month and some said they had a great deal less. Over half the families had pawned possessions in the previous month in order to support themselves and their family (B10). Trying to find up to, and sometimes more than, £50 a day to buy heroin meant that the time and strain involved in doing that rendered parenting difficult, no matter how competent people might otherwise be as parents (B6, B8). Conflict between parents often centred on money worries (B11), with those in treatment finding some welcome relief from such problems (B7). This is not surprising, given the cost of some street drugs. While this varies enormously, as does the amount used, heroin can cost £50 for half a gram, cocaine £40 per gram, and crack cocaine £20 per rock. The link between low income and crime is dealt with in the section on behaviour.

basic care [**AF** - parenting capacity]

Material deprivation in the home was an obvious consequence of some drug use. Furniture and household equipment was not acquired or soon sold. Clothing was not replaced when worn out or too small. Food was not provided, either through lack of cash or because parents neglected to make meals (B12).

ensuring safety [**AF** - parenting capacity]

Drugs or equipment posed physical hazards for children. Parents and other relatives worried about how to store drugs safely, out of reach of children, and how to protect children from seeing parents or other adults using drugs at home (B4, B8). Keeping drugs safe from children was also a problem for stable methadone users who received supplies to last several days (B8). Lack of adequate supervision resulted in children being taken to hospital casualty departments with more serious accidents than other children (B2) and studies included accounts – fortunately rare – of children dying from ingesting their parent's drugs (B7). Part of the problem here was the unrealistic expectations that parents had of their young children – assuming, for instance, that a toddler who had been told not to touch equipment would comply with that command, or expecting children not to copy what they had seen their parents do (B6).

Parents, too, were at risk of accidents. These resulted from dangerous driving whilst under the influence of amphetamines, as well as loss of muscle tone and co-ordination from using opiates and combination drugs that led to parents dropping things and fearing dropping their baby (B6).

stability [**AF** - parenting capacity]

The time and energy needed for acquiring and using drugs could lead to the serious disruption of ordinary household routines. As a result, there might be little stability for many children around mealtimes and bedtimes, getting up and out for school, being washed and cleanly clothed, having fun and recreation, and getting to appointments on time (B11). Parents spoke openly about the chaos of people coming and going at all hours, of children being out late at night with parents looking for drugs, of the home being a mess, and of their guilt – sometimes disgust – at the lifestyle they had inflicted on their children (B12). Unpredictability was a key feature of life, with every day different, depending on how successful or otherwise parents had been at getting their drugs and keeping out of trouble (B11). The impact on children of this unpredictable lifestyle is that they learn that the world is an unstable place, lacking order, structure and planning.

The separation of children and parents – another aspect of instability – is another common theme in the studies. Some separations resulted from parents being away from the home because of residential treatment programmes or custodial sentences (B4, B10, B12). In other cases separation resulted from the disruption of adult relationships that led to one parent or carer leaving the family home.

Or children had been removed and placed with other relatives or with stranger foster carers, usually following intervention by social services. In one study, one in five mothers had had at least one child looked after by the local authority previously, and for an average of 13 months (B10). The proportion was similar in another study, of children on the child protection register, with the parents who used drugs twice as likely as parents not using drugs to be involved in court proceedings, some of which resulted in family separation (B9). For some children the consequence of leaving home meant that they were separated from siblings as well as parents, either because some children remained at home or because siblings were placed separately after leaving home (B12).

neglect [AF - emotional warmth]

A consistent message from the UK studies is that parental drug use increases the likelihood of children being at risk of neglect and emotional abuse, but not other forms of abuse.

Several of the studies have a specific focus on child protection issues and processes and one (B7) examined the evidence for potential harm in the social and physical environment and parental behaviour. One of the child protection studies focused exclusively on children on the local child protection register. Registration was high for neglect and emotional abuse, and heroin use had a very strong correlation with neglect as a professional concern leading to registration. The children of nine out of the ten heroin users were placed on the register for that reason (B9). In the other study with a particular interest in child protection procedures, that of babies treated in hospital for drug withdrawal symptoms, serious concern about neglect – prompting professional intervention and registration – was identified in just over half the study children (B5).

Neglect featured in most of the other studies also. In one, a quarter of the mothers dependent on opiates had children on the child protection register – 13 under the neglect category and the other three for emotional abuse. The mothers had also been taken to court by the local authority – on average twice each – for these child protection concerns (B10).

When parents using amphetamines described the risky situations to which their children were exposed, they included lack of attention in the home, caused by the high drug doses taken by parents (B8). Other parents described specific behaviour as neglectful, such as unsafe storage of drugs and equipment, putting children's need for food and comfort as a lower priority than finding and taking drugs, and snapping at children when feeling low or irritable as the impact of drugs wore off (B7, B11, B12).

In contrast to the above, physical and sexual abuse featured rarely in the studies. There were no reported incidents of either category in the children with withdrawal symptoms at birth (B5), and few in either category in the child protection registration study (B9).

It can be argued perhaps that neglect features in this way because society conceptualises drug use as a neglectful activity. The evidence from parents about what they considered neglectful helps counter this view, although there is no evidence from the child protection registration studies about whether parents agreed with the professionals about the impact of their behaviour on the children.

On balance, the findings overall add weight to the conclusions reported by several researchers in their study write-ups, that some degree of neglect is highly likely in households where resources, both financial and emotional, are invested in the pursuit and use of drugs. The extent of the neglect seems to depend on the relative force, and interaction, of individual, family and social factors. Most parents recognised how adult behaviour resulted in children being neglected, and some were more able or more committed than others to try and protect their children from their own or their partner's lack of care.

The bleak picture painted above is countered, in part, by the range of mitigating factors that emerged in most of the studies that included the views of parents. So, for instance, some of the separations were planned by parents as a way of protecting children from their behaviour. Time was spent with relatives, especially maternal grandmothers, to give children stability and to protect them from seeing their parents' drug use (B1, B4, B6, B8). In addition, all the parents in one study were described as having strategies in mind for protecting their children. These included having rules about not using drugs when children were around, keeping other drug users away from the home, and keeping equipment in places that children could not access (B8). The researchers observed that these strategies worked better for some parents than others.

Finally, going into treatment could act as an important protective factor. Changing from heroin to methadone brought families stability, release from the secret and relentless pursuit of money and drugs, and more time to be with and caring for their children (B4, B8, B20). Researchers commented on the high standards of parental self-care and care of the home and children by heroin users stabilised by methadone (B7).

lessons from other countries - living situation

There is little USA research on the daily experiences of children of drug-using parents, and what there is tends to focus on children placed away from home. It suggests that their experiences differ from those of other separated children in that they tend to enter care earlier, stay longer, and return more often to relatives or friends rather than to their parents. What is not clear is the extent to which these placement decisions stem from the difficulties faced by children or parents rather than from society's attitudes to parents who use drugs.

The USA studies into child maltreatment tend to have a similar starting point as in the UK – using samples of parents referred to welfare agencies or the courts in order to identify the degree and nature of the relationship between parental drug use and child maltreatment. The USA studies produce mixed findings.

In one study, the children of mothers using cocaine were at substantially higher risk of maltreatment – 25 per cent of the children had experienced at least one episode of maltreatment by age two, compared to 4 per cent in the control group. Rates of accidental injury for each group were similar. A second study confounded this finding. Although children of parents using heroin had experienced rates of abuse that were 10 to 15 times higher than the rates for children across the USA, a comparison group of non-drug using families from the same neighbourhood and of similar, low, socio-economic status also had exceptionally high rates of abuse. The findings point to a strong possibility that poverty and other disadvantage may be at the root of the problem and that some disadvantaged families have more resilience than others in coping with adversity.

The findings from USA court samples also need to be considered with caution. Since families under the scrutiny of the state are characterised by high levels of poverty, poor social support, low parental education and a history of maltreatment themselves as children, so drug use may simply be a co-occurring effect caused by an underlying factor.

One study of court files for maltreatment showed that almost half the children had a parent with problem drug (or alcohol) use, but there was no control group matched for socio-economic factors.

A second study is that of Famularo and colleagues and the author is named here because his work is commonly cited in UK reports to evidence the link between specific drugs and specific types of abuse. The study was of court records over a three-year period. Findings indicated that half the children who had been abused sexually had a parent who used cocaine, whilst in half who had been maltreated physically parents used alcohol. There was not, however, any significant association between heroin use and either abuse category. Nor was there any association between maltreatment and the combined effect of parents using more than one drug. No attempt was made to control for socio-economic status or to look at other explanatory factors besides drug use. The research seems most useful in raising questions for further exploration – a point made by Famularo and colleagues in their article (C12) though rarely repeated when their work is reported in the UK.

the impact on family & social relationships

mothers and young children [AF - child's development needs]

Babies born with opiate withdrawal symptoms may need to be separated from their mother for prompt medical attention and for intensive care over several weeks. As a result, the normal process by which mother and baby become attached is constrained. Advice against breast feeding, or the mother's reluctance to do so for fear of harming her baby more, may act as an extra impediment to early bonding (B5).

Other difficulties at the start of the baby's life arise because babies weaned off opiates ingested before birth can be very difficult children to look after. They are irritable, poor feeders and hard to pacify (B5, B6). Commentators suggest that it is the poverty of the mother/baby relationship that is responsible for the most serious effects of maternal drug use in the new-born baby. Similar risks are indicated if drug use during pregnancy has resulted not in opiate withdrawal but in a premature baby or one small for age or born with other problems (B6). Stresses may be compounded if parents feel ill equipped to care for their children – or are deemed by others to be so. What is not evident from these research studies is whether early separation had a long-term impact on maternal and infant bonding, though there is evidence elsewhere of the early difficulties between very low birth weight babies and their carers (C39).

A mother's concern for her unborn or new baby may act as a protective factor. Studies highlight the strong motivation of mothers to act on their concerns for their child once these are understood, including attending ante-natal sessions more regularly and accepting advice that will minimise problems after birth (B6). Mothers expressed relief when their baby was not removed automatically to intensive care (B5) and their deep concern for their baby often led to a new resolve to reduce drug intake (B10). Other studies highlight the varying degrees of success parents achieved in reaching this goal, and the crucial influence of the mother's partner (B6, B7).

parents and older children [AF - child's development needs]

As children grow older, disrupted attachments can occur because of other separations caused by periods in treatment, hospital or prison. Moreover, parents who remain physically at home may not be emotionally available to their children (B4). The recovered heroin users give clear insights into the rebuilding of relationships with children that is an important part of their recovery: putting children before themselves is rewarded, for example by the profound realisation that their children now look forward to seeing them (B12).

A flip side of this emotional distance between parents and children is the role reversal that leads to children being obliged to act as young carers, meeting their parents' need for emotional support. Parents acknowledge and regret this unfair pressure on children that deprives them of normal childhood experiences (B7, B12). Other studies describe the experiences of young carers (C13) but there is a gap in research knowledge about the long-term outcomes for these children.

Other problems may develop between parents and older children. The resolve of parents to be open and honest with children about their own drug use seemed rarely implemented, in part because parents feared that such knowledge would set their children against them (B7). Parents feared rejection because of their lifestyle (B8) and they feared, too, that their failure as a good role model would result in their children adopting their negative patterns of behaviour. This fear was voiced by fathers in particular (B11, B12). Children said they felt angry and resentful towards their parents (B11). None of the studies had a long-enough follow-up period to determine whether the parents' fears materialised.

relationships between parents [AF - child's development needs]

A common thread through the studies is the tension and conflict between parents. In one study, almost half the women living with a partner said they argued a lot and a third reported physical violence (B10). In another study, many of the women were described as living in volatile relationships, with serious domestic violence concerns for some (B5). Individual accounts add detail to the general picture: a woman stopped using drugs when she became pregnant and remained drug free for a further year before reverting to heroin use as relief from her partner's violence (B8). A father described his unstable relationship and the mounting aggression, directed largely at his wife, that resulted from his taking temazepan in increasingly high doses (B7).

Children were affected by their parents' violent relationships. They described the fear of violence as ever present, leading them to try and keep out of the way, or fix things between the adults, or act in a way that would get a good response for themselves, or protect younger siblings from the tension, or escape from home until the conflict had eased (B11).

But not all relationships were tense and negative. One set of studies found many examples of very caring fathers and of men providing an important support system when mothers were coming to terms with the stress of pregnancy and drug use. Researcher observations highlighted the benefit to the children of stable relationships, and mothers spoke positively of the patience of partners with the children and of support for themselves (B7).

Nevertheless, strained relationships were common. Some conflict related directly to drug use, with a particularly close link between the men's drug use and the drug management and health of their partner. In one study, two thirds of the women with a drug-using partner relied on him for her drug supply. Her agreement to reduce her intake, coupled with her partner's support for that commitment, was identified as the most effective influence for positive change. In contrast, her partner's continued use of drugs was the most negative influence – if he used drugs it was likely that she would continue to do so. A significant finding in the study was that although most fathers were pleased about the impending birth of their baby, only one in three of them intended to change their drug habit (B6). In another study the expressed determination of mothers to abstain was not sustained, and none of their partners gave up his drug habit completely (B7).

other relatives [AF - wider family]

Other family members featured as largely positive influences on parents who used drugs. They were closely involved in their life and it was not unusual for relatives to have put pressure on parents to control their habit (B7) or to have helped them make contact with drug treatment services (B8). In the latter study, most parents had access to child care help, mainly from relatives, and in some cases the support was considerable. Grandparents, in particular, played an important role, enabling parents to separate their drug-related activities from their parenting responsibilities. Many older family members were committed to, and supportive of, both their children and their grandchildren, whilst disapproving of the parents' lifestyle (B7).

About half the mothers in this study had a good relationship with their mother, and many others had a good relationship with another female elder such as a maternal aunt or their partner's mother. But there were also strained relationships between the generations. A barrier to parents getting support from relatives was the extent to which drug use was concealed. In one study, the women thought that a third of their mothers and over half of their fathers knew nothing of their drug habit (B6). Others did know and were not supportive. Nearly half the women said they did not confide in, or had no involvement with, their mother. In some cases this might be caused by geographical distance. But in this study the main reason for lack of contact was a breakdown in the relationship, sometimes prompted by disapproval of the parent's drug use and related criminal activity. Other relationship difficulties stemmed from complex and traumatic family histories, with adult children still affected by their parents' divorce and their own childhood experience of injury or other abuse (B6, B12).

other people [AF - family's social integration]

Help to parents to provide adequate care for their children was not limited to family networks only. Friends, too, offered support, again sometimes considerable. But other adults posed risks also and some parents found the social environment as difficult to control as their own habit (B8). Some studies asked parents about their peer relationships – how many friends they had, whether they used drugs, how often they met and where they took drugs. In one study, the majority of parents had friends who also used drugs and some had no friends apart from other drug users. Since most were unemployed, a typical day involved frequent contact and home visits. This was especially the case for amphetamine users who were not in treatment. The hectic social life of these parents diminished only when prolonged heavy use left them more prone to paranoid delusions and aggression. Once in treatment, users tended to become more isolated (B7). The risks to children of parents having frequent contact with other drug users, including taking drugs together in the family home, was acknowledged by parents (B7, B12).

The impact on children's relationships with others was another cause of concern. Children described how their friendships were affected because their caring responsibilities at home left them with little time to socialise or because their feelings of shame about their home circumstances kept them apart from other children. This distance from others was sometimes prompted by the children and sometimes forced on them by other children (B11). And the fear of talking about their home life to other adults such as teachers, who might have been able to offer support, was another burden that left children upset and isolated (B11).

lessons from other countries - family & social relationships

On balance, the following findings chime well with those from the UK studies.

mothers and young children

A USA study concluded that drugs alone did not predict poor-quality interactions between mothers dependent on opiates and their children. What did make a difference was the mother's IQ and socio-economic status and the level of emotional and social support available to her. The implication is that, in the absence of such disadvantages, parenting is unlikely to become problematic.

relationships between parents

Mothers using drugs experienced a high incidence of physical abuse as adults, especially from their partner. In a study of women attending treatment centres, 70 per cent reported being beaten as adults and for 86 per cent of the women this abuse was by their partner.

other people

The impact of social isolation on parents is explored in some USA studies. They find that families experience greater levels of community rejection, with parents less involved in several aspects of social life, including religious, neighbourhood and cultural activities – all of which were identified as protective factors in reducing problem drug use. The sense of exclusion is more pronounced for mothers than fathers – women in heroin treatment were more likely to report that they had no friends, felt lonely and received less social support from friends than either men in treatment or women not using drugs.

children's relationships

USA studies indicate that children of parental drug users have greater problems with peer relationships than other children. They have fewer friends to play with and confide in. They are less confident in their ability to make friends. They are avoided more by their peers. Various factors operate here. In particular, children were ashamed of their parent's drug use, other children were discouraged by parents from mixing with them, and children lacked the social skills to make the right moves. It should be noted that these studies include the use of alcohol as well as other drugs and do not distinguish between the two.

the impact on behaviour

adult behaviour - crime [**AF** - family history and functioning]

The link between parental drug use and criminal activity is a dominant theme in several studies. All 20 mothers with babies treated in hospital for opiate withdrawal symptoms were in contact with the criminal justice system – police, probation, prison – on their own account or because of their partner. Three quarters of the women had been convicted at some time in the past for offences described as drug related, including theft, fraud or prostitution. A quarter of the women had served a prison sentence. All but two of the women had a partner and three quarters of these men had a previous conviction – five for violence, the other eight for theft, drug dealing or drug possession. Five of the men were in prison at the time of the study (B5).

Similar findings emerge from other studies. In one, almost all the mothers (opiate users) had had previous contact with the criminal justice system. Almost three quarters of them had been in prison and two thirds had had a child at that time (B10). In a study of methadone users, with a control group of mothers not on drugs, almost half the methadone users had been in prison, compared with less than a fifth of the control group (B1). The need to steal for drugs was mentioned in several studies (B4, B8, B11, B12).

Two main protective factors were identified in relation to criminal activities. The first was that pregnancy acted as a strong incentive to women to make a break with the past (B8, B9).

The second was the positive impact of methadone maintenance treatment on people's lifestyle. The retrospective analysis of criminal records of 57 patients successfully retained in methadone treatment at two GP surgeries in Sheffield compared their criminal conviction rates and time spent in prison before and after the start of treatment. Overall, patients who persisted with treatment had spent significantly less time in prison than they had before starting treatment (C14). The researchers acknowledge that this may simply reflect the more lenient sentencing by magistrates of offenders who are trying to control their drug use. Whether or not this is true, the point about increased stability remains valid.

adult behaviour - violence [AF - family history and functioning]

Physical violence in the community is another theme in the studies. For the recovered heroin users, this violence had mainly involved other drug users and was often related to disputes about drug transactions, money lending and the purity of drug supplies (B12).

High doses of amphetamines were associated – in another study – with aggression, mainly as a consequence of minor symptoms of delusions. These gave rise to concern because of the deterioration in judgement that at times precipitated unexpected physical attacks by users. (Anecdotally, similar problems are reported for those using cocaine or crack cocaine.) The symptoms were particularly acute when parents were coming down from drugs and the aggression was more marked in women, who tended to react by taking more amphetamines as a way of coping either with the symptoms or with the demands of their children on their time and patience (B7).

Parents were aware of the risks to their children posed by the above circumstances. Their strategies for dealing with these risks included removing themselves from their home or children until things had calmed down, or taking the children to a safer place, especially the home of a relative. They also made occasional use of calming drugs, such as cannabis, as an alternative to taking more stimulants (B7).

Male violence towards female partners, another key theme, was dealt with earlier, in the section on family and social relationships.

children's behaviour [AF - child's developmental needs]

Children were rarely involved directly in their parents' violence with outsiders – only one of the 30 parents who had recovered from heroin described their child being threatened with violence as a lever on his mother to pay her drug debt (B12). But children were involved indirectly, through their exposure to their parents' lifestyle and through knowing that their parents were using drugs. The parents in the above study regretted deeply that they had taken children with them when they went out stealing. Of particular regret was that some children had started copying this behaviour because they had come to consider theft as an acceptable way of life (B12).

Another theme was the aggressive behaviour of children. The shame and resentment they felt towards their parents led some to behave aggressively at home, towards both parents and siblings (B11). Parents felt their children needed help to learn how to control themselves so as not to repeat their own impulsive behaviour (B12).

A related question about behaviour concerns the extent to which parental drug use leads children to use drugs themselves. Three studies raise this issue. Some parents thought it highly likely that children would end up using drugs, either because the children would consider it to be normal behaviour or because drugs would provide an escape from their difficulties (B11). Others said that living in a neighbourhood with high levels of deprivation, drug use and dealing was an added pressure that made children susceptible to drug use. Stopping the drift into drugs was an important reason parents gave for having an open approach with their children about the consequences of using drugs and the need to avoid copying adult behaviour (B7, B8).

lessons from other countries - behaviour

The findings from a USA study about children's behavioural development draw different conclusions about the impact of drug use by mothers and fathers. It found that higher drug involvement by mothers is associated with a decrease in children's obedience and an increase in aggressive, withdrawn and detached behaviour. In contrast, the relationship was not so strong for fathers using drugs, with some reports of positive parenting and greater involvement in activities with their child. The study gives some support for a link between child behaviour and parental drug use – especially in the area of behaviour control. It also, probably, reflects the different roles played by parents in raising children.

Two other sets of studies focus on children's social behaviour: one relates to children living away from home, the other to children still at home. For those children placed away, the findings are mixed. While one study found a distinct pattern of children being anxious in social interactions and showing evidence of both withdrawn behaviour and poor responsiveness to others, the other study found children of drug using parents to be more agreeable, less withdrawn and less tense than other separated children. But the differences were not so great as to count as statistically significant and may be accounted for by the relatively young age at which the children went into care.

In relation to the children still at home, pre-school aged children of mothers on methadone were found to be more impulsive and immature than other children and less able to take responsibility for their actions. In another study, the children of parents dependent on opiates had significantly higher levels of both withdrawn and aggressive behaviour than control groups of children who were either hyperactive or had no psychiatric disorder.

the impact on health – physical and mental

children's health [AF - child's developmental needs]

In the short term at least, children's health is put at risk through the exposure of the foetus to the mother's drug intake. In one study, three of 24 babies were born prematurely (compared to none of the control group of mothers not using drugs) and a third of the babies needed treatment for opiate withdrawal symptoms (B1). In the study of the 20 babies in hospital for their addiction at birth, only three had a significant health problem a year later : one had been severely disabled at birth, one had been hospitalised frequently for a blood disorder and poor weight gain, and the third had poor weight gain and feeding problems (B5). In both studies, therefore, the longer-term prognosis is encouraging. The babies in the second study were predominantly in good health at their first birthday. Those in the first study were, at follow up up to seven years later, as healthy as matched controls (the same applies to their educational development, see later section).

Another health risk for babies is possible contraction of the blood borne viruses that can be transmitted from mother to baby during pregnancy, birth or breast feeding (and between adults through injecting drug use or sexual intercourse). These viruses – Hepatitis B, Hepatitis C and HIV – are all likely to cause ill health later in life. There are useful sections about blood borne viruses in C3 and C15.

As children grow older other health risks may occur. The worry that children might be given drugs by their parents – normally to pacify them – was raised by both children and parents in the family consultation study (B11). And general health precautions might be neglected. In the study of the children of mothers on methadone, their full immunisation rate was 87% compared with 95% in the control group of mothers not using drugs (B1).

A more recent study has examined the health and health surveillance of children of parents attending a drugs treatment centre providing primary health care, and compared them to children in the normal population. The children of the parents using drugs had lower gestational ages at birth, lower birth weights and lower AGPAR scores (the standard test of general well-being at birth). In addition, routine health monitoring and the uptake of immunisations were significantly lower, and many children were not registered with a GP – the treatment centre provided GP support to parents only (B3).

Risk to children's emotional or mental health is another theme raised both by children and adults. Stigma was a major concern. Children were left feeling worthless, ignored by parents whose main preoccupation was the pursuit of drugs, or told to keep home life secret (B8). Another dent to their confidence and self esteem came when peers rejected them because of their unkempt appearance and their parents' anti-social lifestyle (B11). Others were affected by being on the receiving end of their parents' unpredictable behaviour, seeing them sometimes happy and sometimes irritable and, as parents commented, recognising the difference between the two but not understanding it (B12). A current study into local authority care plans for the children of parents with substance misuse problems indicates that a quarter of the children have learning disabilities or mental illness (C16). This figure would, no doubt, be even higher were mental health *problems* and *disorders* – in addition to *illness* – to be included.

parents' health [AF - family history and functioning]

Mental health concerns affected parents too. Three of the 20 babies treated for opiate withdrawal symptoms returned home but were removed permanently a few weeks later. In each case the mother had a history of psychiatric problems. Two had an eating disorder and depression; the other had depression that resulted in a drug overdose (B5). In another study, parents perceived themselves to be in poor health, referring to drug use as an illness that left them feeling helpless, and despised by their neighbours (B11). In a third study, nearly half the mothers had been treated previously for a psychiatric problem, most commonly for depression, and a fifth had had suicidal thoughts (B10).

Depression and irritability were pronounced in another study, of both opiate and amphetamine users, with depression reported by over two-thirds of the sample. Depression was often manifest as insensitivity and emotional unavailability for children, with the impact serious because it affected so many areas of life – basic care, support, guidance and consistency. Irritability and aggression were grave sources of concern for amphetamine users, more so than for those using other drugs. The negative impact on children tended to be about parents using harsh criticism and emotional and verbal abuse (B7).

Pregnancy was a time when motivation to reduce drug use was particularly high. In one study, mothers had tried to reduce their methadone dose levels and the frequency of their use of street drugs but only 17 per cent succeeded in doing so. Some, desperate to protect their babies, reduced their drug consumption too quickly – against advice – and this led to the babies suffering more severe symptoms at birth and, in two cases, to premature delivery (B6).

Parents described the strategies they adopted to reduce or control their health problems. These included not taking drugs each day, or making sure they got enough sleep at night, eating properly, taking iron tablets and generally trying to avoid stress (B7). Others chose not to start methadone treatment for fear of developing an extra addiction on top of their current ones (B4, B8).

A difficulty for parents wanting to control their drug use was their continuing need for the drug as a resource for coping with stressful events or life circumstances. Drugs were a means of getting through difficulties, giving parents the security and confidence to handle stress or the time and patience to cope with the demands of child care. The prognosis for reducing drug intake is low if parents cannot find other – and acceptable – ways of coping with their difficulties (B8).

lessons from other countries - health
children's health

International studies point to children having a higher risk of physical health problems. USA studies suggest that they are more likely than other children to be hospitalised for common childhood illnesses and for minor illnesses. They are also more likely to stay longer in hospital because of staff concerns about their parents' ability to provide care and cope with stress. A Spanish study of the children of injecting heroin users analysed the children's hospital records. The children were more prone to developing illnesses than those with non-heroin using parents, with the most common ones being infectious and nutritional diseases and those related to parental neglect or disinterest. It is noted that over half the mothers using heroin were young parents still in their teens, possibly implying that parental age should have been used when determining the control group.

Other studies provide evidence that children of drug using parents are at higher risk for symptoms of depression and anxiety, using standardised scales to compare them with children of parents not using drugs. But, though the risk was increased, the results did not amount to clinical depression or anxiety.

parents' health

USA studies indicate that both opiate and cocaine users are likely to have a co-existing psychiatric disorder when they present for treatment. Among opiate users there is a high incidence of mood and anxiety disorders and high rates of depression. Cocaine users are found to have significantly high rates of emotional disorders. But it is difficult to disentangle cause and effect in these studies. It is not clear whether psychiatric symptoms develop from the effects and lifestyle associated with drug use or whether drugs have been used to treat psychiatric symptoms. Either way, the combination of mental health problems and drug use may be associated with greater parenting difficulties among those using drugs.

the impact on education [AF - education]

The UK studies have very little to say about the developmental outcomes for children of parents using drugs, bar a general acknowledgement that it is difficult to disentangle the relative influence of drug exposure from the other environmental factors which impinge on children's lives. While both are thought to be relevant, the degree of influence of each is hard to determine.

Children in the family consultation study provided vivid accounts of how play and leisure opportunities were dented by their parents' behaviour. Children were prevented from playing out with friends, or made to keep quiet indoors, or denied the chance to play with other children if parents excluded them from the home (B11). The fear of children's development being set back if they were ostracised by others was voiced by parents in some studies (B8, B11).

Language and cognitive development featured specifically in two studies. A father, worried about his child's poor speech development, attributed his slow progress to the fact that the neighbours refused to let their children mix with him (B7). In the other study, of mothers on methadone treatment, the children had similar scores on behaviour and development to the control group of children with mothers not using drugs. The slightly reduced head growth of the children exposed to opiates did not appear to be having a negative impact on their intellectual functioning when they were tested up to seven years after birth (B1).

There was more reference to the likely and actual impact of children's functioning at school – it featured in all studies including children of school age. Starting school brought into sharp relief the conflict for some children between, on the one hand, the need to integrate with their peers and, on the other, a sense of loyalty to parents. Children felt different from others in class or the playground because of their exposure to both the use of drugs and to conversations about drugs. In addition, they had been told not to talk about their parents' behaviour and were reluctant to invite others to their home (B7). The Irish study, with its comparison group, highlights the relationship between poor school progress and home circumstances (B4).

Parents feared their children would be isolated at school, or teased or bullied for their parents' lifestyle (B7, B8, B12). They worried that children who had lost respect for their parents, because of drug use, would react by behaving badly and – if this happened at school – would run the risk of being excluded (B11). Some children missed school because they were kept at home to care for parents and siblings, or because they had no clean clothes or had not had head lice treated, or because the children did not want to go to school and parents did not press them to do so (B4, B7).

Parents acknowledged these difficulties and had strategies to overcome them. Some mothers were vigorous in their efforts to keep their drug use hidden from the children, in order to ensure that the children would be accepted outside the home (B7). The evidence from other studies is that children often knew what their parents were trying to keep secret (B7, B11). Other mothers resolved to reduce their drug use by the time children started nursery or school (B8). Children said that school was important, partly as a way of escaping their home situation, but they felt reluctant to confide in teachers and others who might be a source of support. Parents thought school was important, to help children develop their abilities and also break free from their impoverished surroundings (B11).

lessons from other countries - education

The findings from USA studies provide a degree of consistency about children's education – they point to problematic outcomes for the cognitive development of children compared with children in their neighbourhood whose parents do not use drugs. In one study, children of fathers using heroin were at greater risk for poor school progress. They scored lower on tests for IQ and perceptual-motor performance and had a greater need for remedial teaching. They also had more behaviour problems at school, were absent more often, and were more likely to have their parents contacted because of the children's misbehaviour.

A second study, also of fathers using heroin, found that almost half the children exhibited slower mental development than the control children. Children in a third study scored significantly lower on a test of arithmetic but not on reading or spelling. And, in the fourth study – both a small pilot and a larger replication exercise – pre-school children of mothers on methadone treatment performed significantly worse on tests for IQ, though their scores fell within the normal range.

Whilst these studies focus on differences between children of parents using or not using drugs, others have explored the relative impact of drugs as opposed to other environmental influences. One compared children exposed to drugs before birth with three different control groups – children whose mothers were using drugs now but had not done so when pregnant, children at high risk because of medical complications at birth, and children with a similar (low) socio-economic status as the experimental group. The children were tested for physical, intellectual, sensori-motor and behavioural development. The children exposed pre-natally performed significantly worse than the rest, and the children with mothers now on drugs did significantly less well than the other two groups. Such results provide evidence of a strong effect from the child-rearing environment as well as of a biological effect from drug exposure before birth.

some messages for practice

There are very few UK studies that describe service interventions for parents using drugs and none of them includes robust evaluation of the service described. But lessons about practice can be drawn from the family experiences described earlier and so this final section draws on both types of study – impact as well as intervention. The section also draws on some USA studies about interventions with drug-using parents because their clear focus on measuring change in families' lives have important messages about both the content and the style of service delivery.

Some of the key messages for practice are about:
- clarity about needs – locality and individual
- services acceptable to parents
- direct work with children
- work with fathers as well as mothers
- support for the extended family
- professional attitudes.

clarity about needs - locality and individual

There are two sides to assessing needs – one is about understanding the local picture and getting a sense of what can be achieved and how, the other is about assessing the needs of individual children and parents.

locality need [including outcomes and services]

Various methodologies can be used for auditing community needs, including the Matching Needs and Services planning tool described elsewhere (C2, C17). Whichever tool is preferred, planners need to focus on four key elements:
- First, identify need – what are the needs of children and their families when parents have problem drug use?
- Second, specify outcomes – how do we want the lives of the children and parents to be different as a result of our responding to the needs identified?
- Third, use research – what does the research evidence tell us about interventions that are effective in achieving the desired outcomes?
- Fourth, develop and implement services – what service model should be designed, based on the local audit of need and other research evidence? Should it be implemented by commissioning new services or reconfiguring existing ones? What evaluation will help us identify whether it works?

A model service specification for problem substance use is set out in another booklet in this series (C2). The focus there is on parental problem drinking, but the specification can be adapted for problem drug use.

Conducting this audit and planning work as a multi-agency exercise will increase the chances of local ownership of the data assembled and the ideas generated. It should help increase awareness of the sort of services currently available and likely to be useful – research in one authority into the impact of parental substance misuse on caseloads found that social workers were often unsure of what would support families better (A3). And including the perspectives of service users will increase the chances of developing services that will be welcomed and used. An example of one borough's audit, service planning around drug (and alcohol) misuse, and parental involvement can be found in C18.

individual need [including risk and protective factors]

The starting point for sensitive practitioners is that parents want the best for their children and the fact that parents use drugs does not mean that they do not care about, and cannot care for, their children (B4, B8). But, if concerns are raised – by families or professionals – there is something to be assessed, and this needs to be done in a measured way, without either ignoring or over reacting to the drug use. The important point is not to make assumptions about the impact of drug use and not to generalise about people's circumstances (B8, C19).

A useful approach to assessment is provided by a model that deems intervention necessary if the parent's drug use and style of parenting exaggerates parenting problems, in circumstances where there is a high level of demand on the parent for parenting, and where there are few other resources to help supplement what they can offer (C20). Four questions are explored in turn, in order to make a judgement about whether intervention is needed.

- First, what is the place of drugs in the parent's life? – which drugs, how and when obtained, at what cost, how and when taken, with whom, in what circumstances.
- Second, what are the effects of drugs on the parent? – on their availability as parents and on their display of affection and their use of control and discipline.
- Third, what is the impact on the child of this style of parenting? – how well is the child's need for basic care, protection, stimulation and love being met.
- Fourth, does the parent have to provide for all the child's needs? – are others available to share this responsibility.

This approach chimes well with the requirement under the Assessment Framework for Children in Need to conduct assessments which focus on the child's developmental needs, on parenting capacity and on family and environmental factors (C1). In essence, it provides for an evaluation of the risk and protective factors in children's lives. The literature about which children are likely to cope well, despite adverse circumstances, including problem drug use by parents, all points in the same direction (C21, C22). Key factors identified by researchers include:

- child – self-esteem, sociability and autonomy
- family – compassion, warmth and absence of parental discord
- environment – social support systems in school and the community that encourage personal effort and coping.

One of the most difficult dilemmas facing practitioners is having to weigh up, on the one hand, strong emotional attachments between parents and children and, on the other, chronic poor care and neglectful actions or omissions (B6). An added complicating factor may be the time needed for parents to make changes. Where drug use is chaotic, enduring and dependant, practitioners may be fighting a losing battle offering services to keep children in the parental home. But keeping them within their family network might well be possible, especially if the messages from the research studies about building on the goodwill and commitment of other relatives is heeded. And intensive programmes that offer families services that are accessible and welcoming can enable children to remain safely at home, sometimes against all the odds (B21).

services acceptable to parents

There is a clear message from the research studies that parents will use services they find acceptable and will avoid those they don't. If agencies are to maximise the chances of achieving better outcomes for children, they need to listen to what parents say about the services they would want to use. This includes the following:

practical help with the stresses on parents

The research studies highlight the extent to which parents use drugs to help them feel more able to cope with life's difficulties. Many parents were self-medicating with drugs their problems of depression, anxiety, irritability and lack of coping skills (B7). They needed to reduce those stresses, or find other ways of coping, before they could succeed in reducing their problem drug use. For some, the stresses were about parenting, housing or finances. Others were troubled by past or present relationships, especially those with partners, and in particular those which involved domestic violence. And worries about children – especially health, behaviour and schooling – were a recurring theme (B8, B13, B22). The outreach work attached to one intervention project was used mainly for transporting children and parents to important appointments, for facilitating family activities, and for escorting children to school. The latter enabled a child to return to school after several months' absence and gave his mother time to re-establish family routines (B22).

Mental health worries were another major concern, as was alcohol use in combination with other drugs. The co-existence of adult substance misuse and mental health problems (often described as 'comorbidity' or 'dual diagnosis') found in these studies adds weight to what is already known about the consequences for adults and those close to them. New guidance that urges mental health teams to offer integral treatment to those using drugs should help remedy some of the unhelpful divisions between current services (C23).

What parents wanted was help to sort out life's problems. They valued having someone to talk to, someone to help lighten the load, someone to suggest practical ways of dealing with problems, to point them in the right direction (B4, B8, B13, B22). The USA treatment studies with a focus on parenting, using existing training material adapted for drug misusing parents, have been successful in improving parental confidence and behaviour as well as reducing drug use and domestic conflict (B15, B18). An initiative in one London borough is promoting this approach, offering a parenting course for adult family members with experience of drug use and run by facilitators trained in substance misuse issues and – in some cases – with drug experience themselves (C24).

Adapting course materials for the target audience is of key importance in engaging parents. In the USA, a family skills training programme with reported success with drug using parents was modified for use with an African-American urban population (B14). In the UK, the Race Equality Unit has adapted a different USA parenting programme for minority ethnic communities here. This work was prompted by the failure of family centres to make their parent education programmes relevant to black and minority ethnic parents (C25). The programme that has been developed (C26) is being piloted with groups of parents with problematic drug use.

reduce isolation

Women, in particular, were at risk of social isolation. It was not uncommon for pregnant women to have only partners and relatives to rely on for social support (B7). Others wishing to become or remain drug free needed to avoid the people and places that might tempt them to relapse (B8). What was wanted was the opportunity to get involved in neighbourhood, cultural, religious or other activities that might open the door to new networks. For parents reluctant to use services that are generally available, lest their past or current drug use results in rejection, specific services may help them explore new friendships without this fear. Others may prefer to join groups where people have other things in common – such as age, gender, ethnicity or neighbourhood – but can use the meetings as an opportunity to deal with their problems, including those linked to drug use (B16, B21). Studies of domestic violence point to the particular importance of outreach and advocacy services for women who have experienced fear and isolation (C37).

build on parental motivation

Becoming a parent can act as a trigger to make lifestyle changes and, for those using drugs, it may provide the incentive to reduce their intake. Pregnant women wanted non-judgemental help and advice about how to look after their unborn child and themselves. The period just after birth is a particularly important time to boost a mother's determination. Extra reassurance and practical support will be especially helpful for mothers with babies born with drug withdrawal symptoms, so that strong attachments can be nurtured with these babies whose irritability can make it so difficult to care for them. Important here is the need to take the lead from parents about what they believe to be good measures of their success. Realistic outcomes are more likely to be achieved than over-optimistic expectations. Care needs to be taken so that parents do not set themselves up to fail. Parents may be desperate to stop using drugs, but lacking the confidence to do so (B22). Drug reduction or control may achieve stability for families who might otherwise not make progress if the goal were to stop using drugs altogether.

Timing is important. Delays in getting help can mean that opportunities to build on motivation are lost or – at the extreme – that parents get themselves arrested, in the hope that they will then get referred for priority treatment (B13). Timing is crucial, too, in helping keep people engaged with services (B21, B22). One of the USA studies attributed its success in completing a high proportion of health and development checks on the children of the parents in treatment to its vigilance in encouraging attendance – including a letter sent a week before the appointment, a verbal reminder the day before, transport on the day, a non-punitive response to missed appointments, and a willingness to reschedule appointments as many times as necessary (B17).

build on existing services

Parents wanted services that would take account of their child care responsibilities and their busy lifestyle, in part the result of having to visit so many agencies that it felt like a full-time job (B13, B22). They would have preferred more home visits, with the advantage that would bring of being able to meet workers in privacy. Safety was an issue, too, with parents worrying about having to take children with them to meetings with drug workers and probation officers. And they worried about what to do if they could not keep children with them whilst getting treatment (B22). There is a message here about what priority, if any, agencies give to making adult drug services child friendly.

Parents who are attending treatment centres might be encouraged to bring their children with them, and professional staff might be encouraged to extend their work beyond drug control, to include work on parent-child relationships and attending to any special health or other needs of children. Such an approach in the USA, at two out-patient methadone clinics, succeeded in getting both basic and specialist follow-up attention to children's health and development needs (B17). Checks were completed on 85 per cent of the children, as opposed to only 10 per cent when parents had to take their children to a separate health centre. The results compare favourably with the experience of London parents whose children's basic health needs were overlooked when parents could not access services for them at the centre that they, as adult drug users, used (B3).

In-patient or residential services might adopt a similar inclusive approach. The findings of one of the UK studies suggests that we can be cautiously optimistic about treating parental drug use in a residential family-based environment – in the short term, at least, the outcomes for adults compared favourably with the published results for adults in residential centres which did not include children (B20).

Developments of this nature cannot succeed without positive liaison between different disciplines and between adult and children's services. This was an explicit aim of one of the USA studies, delivering parenting training to mothers in treatment (B18), and it was deemed essential for the success of the children's programme at parental out-patient clinics, as described above (B17). There are examples of good practice along these lines being developed in the UK. One offered parents misusing drugs a one-stop shop, at a local family centre, for health and other services to help them continue caring for their children (B21). Another two deal with alcohol as well as drug misuse. They provide a link worker for families where there are substance misuse and child care issues, in one case through a specialist practitioner who divides her time between the child care office and the adult drugs and alcohol centre (B22) and in the other through a practitioner based in the social services family centre (C18).

These pilot models vary in their detail but have key factors in common: an intensive approach with an emphasis on outreach work with families, specialist drug workers charged with fostering positive links across local agencies, and a commitment to take a holistic view of what is needed, rather than responding in a crisis in ways that may resolve the immediate and temporary need but leaves other needs unattended.

Schools provide another focus of support – to build on parental concerns about their children's achievement and relationships with other children and to offer direct help to children from a familiar base. The opportunities they provide need to be exploited (C38).

direct work with children

Where parental drug use is problematic, children need opportunities to both understand and escape from the stresses they experience. Parents are as aware of these needs as professionals (B4, B22).

Children acting as young carers may need reassurance that they are not to blame for their parents' problems and that it is not their responsibility to resolve adult conflict or take on a caring role that is beyond their years. Help may be needed to cope with the losses they suffer – when they have to stay away from home, or when parents are in treatment or prison or have left home. Some may need reassurance that they will not be removed from their family, especially if they have picked up on their parents' fear that this might happen.

One way of responding to these needs is to provide children with opportunities for group discussion and activities, though an exclusive focus on families affected by problem drug use may not be the best approach. It may be difficult to attract children who are living at home, and the small numbers recruited may mean trying to work with children of very different ages, abilities and interests (B21). An alternative approach is to have more general play and leisure opportunities – parents are more likely to agree this sort of activity and children are more likely to choose it for themselves. Having fun and recreation, in a safe place in the community, and under the supervision of adults attuned to the differing special needs of the children, may well succeed on three counts – enabling children to enjoy themselves, to improve their social skills with their peers, and to gain the confidence to discuss their worries with trusted adults. Examples of such community development approaches are given in A4.

Another aspect of direct work with children is help to cope with the changes at home that are consequent on parents benefiting from drug and parenting programmes. Whilst parent training programmes can succeed in having an impact on the behaviour of very young children, they are less effective with older children who may resent and resist parents' attempts to impose new rules and boundaries (B15). What seems to work better is separate work with the children to help them develop their own problem-solving skills and new ways of coping with stress (B14) or joint sessions of both parents and children. Specialised, and intensive, programmes that focus on entrenched parent-child interactions may also be useful. In the USA, multi-systemic therapy has had positive results in reducing children's anti-social behaviour, including in families where problem drug use is an issue for parents as well as children (A4, C27).

work with fathers as well as mothers

There are clear messages in the research studies about the crucial influence of men, both as fathers and as partners. This is welcome, and should help guard against the exclusive focus on mothers that tends to occur in social care work. The positive support given by partners was valued by women trying to reduce their use of drugs during pregnancy, and mothers described how the care of children was eased when both parents shared that task.

A more difficult message to convey to men is the importance of their own drug status. Babies born with drug withdrawal symptoms were more likely to remain with their mother if her partner was either free from drugs or in treatment. Similarly, the most effective influence for positive change in maternal drug use was the woman's agreement to reduce her intake coupled with support from her partner. The most negative influence was her partner's continued use of drugs (B8). But the finding in more than one study was that, although partners were pleased at the prospect of becoming a father, few intended or succeeded in reducing their drug use.

Promoting the more active, and positive, involvement of men is a challenge for practice. The commitment and personal skills of individual workers are ingredients that can help convey to fathers that their involvement in child rearing is both necessary and desirable (B14, B21). But this needs to be addressed pro-actively, as a staffing and recruitment issue, rather than being left to chance. It might also benefit from trying different ways of involving fathers – and other family members – in planning for children's welfare and safety. The Family Group Conference model, which starts from the premise that families know their children best and can make good decisions for them, is an option to pursue (C28).

A similarly pro-active stance needs to be taken in relation to working with men whose relationship with their partner is violent or conflictual. The USA programme that had a positive effect on domestic conflict, as well as on parenting skills, rule setting and drug use, included anger management and communication techniques in its intensive programme of family training and home-based follow-up work (B15). UK services for domestic violence, anger management and parenting for fathers are described in C29. The particular issues for domestic violence and substance misuse are reviewed in C30.

support for the extended family

The supportive role played by relatives – especially grandparents – emerges as a consistent theme in the studies. Grandparents put pressure on parents to control their use of drugs. They persuaded some to seek help from services. They cared for children during periods when parents were unable to do so. These informal, or formal foster care, arrangements were not necessarily free of tension. Relationships could be fraught, because of past family difficulties, because the elders disapproved of their children's drug use, because of disputes around contact with the other side of the family, or because parents felt guilty or uneasy seeing their parents doing a better job than themselves of caring for their children.

There are two clear messages for practice. One is about the value of exploring and using family strengths when planning for children. It is an important protective factor to build on. The other is about avoiding the assumption that relatives can cope alone. While many can and do, others will welcome or need professional help to capitalise on their goodwill. Specific information may be needed, about different drugs, about patterns of drug use that are harmful and harm free, or about the possibility of their children changing their drug use and the likely timescales involved.

Counselling, or other emotional support, has been found useful in helping family members generate solutions to problems, including coping with actual or potentially stressful events or circumstances such as contact, custody and family conflict (C31, C32). Relatives may need to help the children cope with difficult situations, too, and some may welcome practical help with parenting issues, especially if it is some time since they cared for young relatives, or if children have emotional or behavioural difficulties (B4, B13).

And financial support needs to be adequate. Local authorities should bear in mind two recent court cases, both applications for judicial review of a local authority's policy to pay short-term foster carers who are relatives or friends a lower rate than that paid to other foster carers (C33). The judge described the policy as unlawful, irrational and fundamentally discriminatory, fixing – as it did – an arbitrary and inflexible cash limit that was so low as to put it in conflict with the welfare principle. The policy was further criticised for being neither formulated nor exercised according to the needs of the children and for operating as a disincentive to relatives and friends to become carers. This was deemed contrary to the Children Act principle of placing children with family members, where possible, and contrary to the generally held view that there is value in placing children within their own family.

professional attitudes

Practitioners and policy makers need to be vigilant about the biases they bring to their work. For example, mothers who have problem drug use may be viewed with more criticism than would be evoked by similar behaviour in men. Parents who use drugs may be viewed with suspicion, as if drug use equates with inadequate parenting. And the opportunity to offer help may be lost because of wrong assumptions that drug use is not a problem in certain minority ethnic groups (C34). The important thing is to look at people's behaviour, not at the label that society attaches to them.

An open approach to parents will increase the chances of them having confidence in the help on offer. As the UK and Irish studies show, many parents well understand the negative impact of problem drug use on children. They know when they need help, and they feel guilty and ashamed if children have been neglected. But they live, too, with the fear that their children may be removed from them – this was the most commonly expressed concern of parents in one study (B8).

Wary of contact with services, they are sensitive to how they are treated by professionals. Many parents in the studies were appreciative of individual workers whom they saw as allies in their life (B7, B8). They were critical of workers whom they felt were patronising or who held back from offering support because of their drug use. GPs in particular tended to be singled out for such criticism (B8, B22), reflecting – no doubt – the doctors' own lack of confidence in working with patients using drugs (C35).

A sensitive response by workers will include an acknowledgement of their strengths as parents, a focus on the issues they want to work on, and a willingness to provide a flexible solution that takes account of their particular life style, experience and drug use. A real understanding of the dilemmas faced by parents is important. The impact of the cost of some drugs on family life should not be under-estimated. Nor should the stability to children's lives that many parents seem to achieve when they control rather than try to stop using drugs altogether. Since professionals, like others in society, are likely to be influenced by the illegality of some drug use and some related behaviour, a move in the direction of legal reform might also have an impact on attitudes to parents using drugs.

summaries of studies

the nature of the evidence

A note of caution should be sounded about the weaknesses of much of current social care research. Some of the following points relate specifically to problem drug use whilst others are more general.

- The bulk of research studies are from the USA. Care should be taken before generalising from one place to another, though this is not to say that no lessons can be drawn from experience elsewhere. One particular difference between the USA and the UK and Irish contexts relates to the types of drugs, with cocaine the preferred drug of choice for more USA than UK and Irish parents with problem use. Another difference concerns the policy response to drug use. In some USA states court intervention in the recent past on the grounds of child neglect was begun automatically following the birth of a baby suffering opiate withdrawal, irrespective of the family's ability to care for their child. Research studies that rely on court records may not produce findings that are relevant to places with a different policy approach.

- There is variation in the use of terms to describe the problems being researched and a lack of definition about the meaning of words such as 'drug exposure', 'drug affected', 'addicted' as well as 'use', 'misuse' and 'abuse'. This makes it difficult to be clear about the nature and severity of problems and to compare findings from different studies.

- There is a disproportionate focus on research into pregnancy and the foetus and newborn baby as opposed to the impact at later stages of development. This reflects the medical interest underpinning much of the USA research into drug use and the greater ease in tracking this group of drug users.

- It follows from the above that there is little attention paid to the outcomes for children in terms of their social, emotional, behavioural and educational development. The absence of comparison or control groups in most studies makes it impossible to tease out the relative impact on parenting of problem drug use as opposed to environmental factors such as poverty, discrimination and educational and other disadvantage. The lack of longitudinal studies – that track children over time – leaves us uncertain about how children's lives unfold when parents use drugs.

- There is a lack of published research on drug use in black and minority ethnic communities, its impact on children, and how this might differ from the experience of white communities. In addition, even some recent studies fail to explain the ethnic composition of the people in their research sample.

- Many parents are polydrug users, and drugs affect people differently. It is difficult to disentangle the relative impact of different drugs in samples that include parents using more than one drug.
- Nor does research help us understand the impact on children of the different stages of a parent's problem drug use – when use is becoming serious, when parents are in treatment, when they relapse, when they recover.
- Research is not neutral. Researchers are not free of the biases in society towards parental attitudes and behaviour. Given the popular negative assumptions made about drugs and parenting, there may be a tendency to emphasise deficits in parents rather than competence.

These problems are highlighted, not to deter social care professionals from reading and using the research studies reviewed here or elsewhere, but to remind readers that they need to approach research with an enquiring mind. Research does not provide the 'right answer', only evidence to be considered alongside other information. And there will always be a place for practitioners and commissioners to add their experience to what is already available, by building robust evaluation into their service plans.

summary chart of impact and intervention studies

impact studies - with control group

Ref.	Date	Author
B1	1996	Burns, O'Driscoll & Watson
B2	1998	Alison & Wyatt
B3	2000	Jayasooriya
B4	2001*	Hogan & Higgins

impact studies - no control group

B5	1995 *	Powell
B6	1998 *	Klee & Jackson
B7	1998 *	Centre for Social Research on Health and Substance Abuse (SRHSA)
B8	1998 *	Elliott & Watson
B9	2000	Forrester
B10	2000 *	Powis, Gossop, Bury, Payne & Griffiths
B11	2001 *	Mahoney & MacKechnie
B12	2002 *	McKeganey, Barnard & McIntosh
B13	2001 *	Kearney & Taylor

intervention studies - with control group

B14 (USA)	1996 *	Aktan, Kumpfer & Turner
B15 (USA)	1999 *	Catalano, Gainey, Fleming, Haggerty & Johnson

intervention studies - no control group

B16 (USA)	2000 *	McCartt Hess, McGowan & Botsko
B17 (USA)	2000 *	Shulman, Shapira & Hirshfield
B18 (USA)	2001 *	Moore & Finkelstein
B19	1991 *	Kearney & Ibbetson
B20	2000	Keen, Oliver, Rowse & Mathers
B21	2002 *	Harbin
B22	2002 *	Hayden, Jerrim & Pike

* indicates a particular focus on family experiences and outcomes

B1
Burns, O'Driscoll & Watson
1996, W. London Hospital

drug/s
· Heroin or methadone during pregnancy.
· Currently in methadone maintenance treatment.
· Just under half of partners also on opiates.

sample and methods
· 23 children of mothers attending local drug dependency unit.
· Aged 3-7.5yrs when study conducted.
· 57% white, 17% Black African, 9% mixed race, 7% ethnicity unknown.
· Control group – 20 children matched for age, and social class as determined by housing type.

what was studied
· Medical examination – child's head circumference, height.
· Developmental test – child's locomotor, social, manipulative, communication skills.
· Child behaviour – questionnaire completed by mother.

key findings
· The head size of the treatment group was smaller, but there were no differences in the health and development scores between treatment group and control group.
· Researchers link good outcomes for treatment group to, possibly:
· stability from methadone treatment
· help from treatment unit
· mothers being stable, long-term drug users.

B2
Alison & Wyatt
1998, Sheffield Hospital

drug/s
· Illicit drugs or methadone during pregnancy.

sample and methods
· 48 children of mothers who informed neonatal services of drugs taken during pregnancy.
· 4 groups – recreational users, those who stopped early in pregnancy, those on controlled daily methadone dose, heroin/cocaine users.
· Children aged 18 months – 5 years at study.
· Control group – 48 children matched on age and postcode.
· Mothers similar in age, ethnicity and Townsend scores of deprivation.

what was studied
· Involvement in child protection procedures.
· Whether child cared for by someone other than mother, including foster care, adoption, other.
· Take up of routine health and developmental checks.

key findings
· Children of mothers on methadone were as likely to be involved in child protection procedures as heroin/cocaine users.
· Most of the initial child protection conferences were held because of concerns arising from actual neglect rather than as routine post-birth planning meetings.
· Babies born with withdrawal symptoms were more likely than others to be placed away from the mother.
· Researchers link poor outcomes for mothers on methadone to possibly:
· changing drug taking habits of mothers
· changes in domestic situation.
· new drug-using partners.

B3
Jayasooriya
2000, London

drug/s
· 80% of mothers were using methadone at registration with the GP unit.
· 70% used heroin, mainly by injecting.
· 25% used cocaine or diazepam.

sample and methods
· 55 children born over a 4 year period to mothers using an NHS GP unit for drug users in contact with local drug treatment agencies.
· Review of health and social services records.
· Ethnic origin was not recorded for half the study group. All but 2 of those recorded were white.
· Control group – a local group of children from the same birth cohort, matched for age and (where possible) ethnicity.

what was studied
· How the children accessed primary health care services (as they were not available from the specialist GP unit used by their mother).
· Health scores at birth and in infancy.
· Level and nature of contact with health professionals.

key findings
· The children of mothers using drugs had significantly lower gestational ages at birth, lower birth weights and lower AGPAR scores.
· The uptake of immunisations and routine health monitoring was significantly lower for the study group.
· Many of the study children were not registered with a GP, in part because it was wrongly assumed by professionals that the mothers' GP cared for them.

B4
Hogan & Higgins
2001, Dublin, Ireland

drug/s
· Heroin, methadone, other opiates.
· 74% were or had been regular drug injectors and 80% used more than one type of opiate regularly.
· 74% were receiving treatment, including 68% on methadone.

sample and methods
· 50 families with at least one parent using opiates. The study child was their oldest child of primary school age, in their care for most of the previous year.
· Two Dublin locations with high levels of opiate use & unemployment.
· Interviews with parents (68 mothers & 32 fathers), 2 focus groups with professionals, and survey questionnaire of the study child's teachers.
· Control group - 50 families from the same areas, with similar socio-economic background, age and sex of study child, but with neither parent using drugs since child's birth.

what was studied
· Impact of parental opiate use on children's family life - including the experience of care by parents, exposure to drugs-related lifestyle, social-emotional well being, academic progress and social support systems.

key findings
· Strains of living with disadvantage can be greatly increased by drug use, but there is much variation in the circumstances and responses of both parents and children.
· Children of drug-using parents tended to have more academic and behavioural difficulties. Gaps in learning caused by worry and poor concentration difficult to redress.
· Relatives provided continuity and stability for children but were largely unsupported in a difficult role.
· Drug treatment services were perceived as focusing on drug users as individuals rather than family members with responsibilities and relationships.

B5
Powell
1995, Inner London Hospital

drug/s
· 75% mothers on methadone, the others had refused it.
· Only 20% mothers used only heroin or methadone.
· Most mothers had had long period of drug use before pregnancy.
· Of 14 partners, 6 were in treatment, 4 had detoxed, 4 had not used drugs.

sample and methods
· 20 babies treated for drug withdrawal symptoms at birth.
· Review of hospital records and information from involved professionals up to one year later.

what was studied
· The outcomes for children.
· Useful factors in the assessment of drug-using parents.
· Child protection issues relevant to drug-using parents.

key findings
· Good outcomes (still at home after 1 year and no child care concerns) were associated with :
· mothers having stable drug use
· mothers being in treatment
· mothers having had good ante-natal care
· in permanent accommodation
· with a partner free from drugs or in treatment.
· Poor outcomes (permanent removal of the baby at birth or later) were associated with:
· maternal psychiatric problems
· removal of, or continuing concern about, another child in the home
· domestic violence and/or other instability in personal relationships
· chaotic drug use which parents were unable or unwilling to control.

B6
Klee & Jackson
1998, N.W.England (Manchester, Liverpool and other large urban areas)

drugs
· The women were polydrug users.
· Most used heroin as preferred drug, and high proportion injected.
· Over half of partners used heroin or morphine, mostly injecting.

sample and methods
· 64 pregnant drug users (reducing to 50 by final interview) recruited through drug agencies, ante-natal clinics, drug outreach workers and community networks (part of the B7 study).
· 4 semi-structured interviews conducted over 12-18 months: during pregnancy, soon after birth, 6 months later, 12 months after that.

what was studied
· The clinical and social problems faced by pregnant drug users and mothers.
· Their needs, and experiences of using services.

key findings
· Most of the women tried to reduce their drug intake when pregnant.
· They were more successful after the baby's birth.
· They were less successful if their partners continued to use drugs and if they perceived health professionals to be negative towards them.
· Most of the women had had mental health problems in the past, usually stemming from childhood experiences.
· Some maternal grandmothers provided good support to their daughters and grandchildren.

B7
Centre for Social Research on Health and Substance Abuse (SRHSA)
1998, N.W.England

drug/s
· Amphetamine users.
· Polydrug users.
· Pregnant women (in B6).

sample and methods
· 221 parents involved in 3 different studies by the Research Centre during 1990 – 1997.
· Just under half were fathers.
· The children ranged from babies to young adults.
· Semi-structured interviews with parents, mainly in their home, plus information from field notes and researcher discussions.

what was studied
· The attitudes, behaviour and approaches to parenting of drug-using parents.
· The hazards for children and the awareness and responsiveness of parents.
· Parents' efforts to protect their children from harm.
· The risk and protective factors in the physical environment and social context of children's lives.

key findings
· Parents acknowledged and regretted the pressure children were under to care for their parents.
· The strategies parents used to protect their children from harm included removing either themselves or the children from the home until it was safe to return.
· Harsh criticism and emotional and verbal abuse were seen as having a negative impact on children.
· Parents worried that their lifestyle would leave their children at a disadvantage when socialising at school and in the community.
· Parents with supportive partners and/or relatives were more able to remove or lessen the adverse impact of their drug use on the children.
· Grandparents, in particular, exerted a largely positive influence, supporting their grandchildren without approving of their parents' lifestyle.

B8
Elliott & Watson
1998, N.W.England (Salford and Trafford)

drug/s
· Heroin was the preferred drug of choice, with crack cocaine the second.
· A high proportion were polydrug users, taking 4 or more drugs at the time of study.

sample and methods
· 52 parents who were using drugs.
· An even mix of mothers and fathers.
· Children were aged 1-10 years.
· Some parents were receiving services, others were not.
· Semi-structured interviews, some conducted by former or stable drug users trained by the research team.

what was studied
· How being a parent impacted on people's use of drugs and drug services, in order to provide information about needs to the local Drug Action Team.

key findings
· Parents were clear about the possible impact of drug use on their children and wanted to protect their children from negative experiences.
· Relatives, especially grandparents, were an important source of support for parents and their children.
· Services need to be flexible and sensitive to the wide diversity of life styles and needs resulting from different parenting experiences and drug use.

B9
Forrester
2000, Inner London

drug/s
· 10 families where parent/s deemed by social worker to be using heroin.
· 1 family where parent/s deemed by social worker to be using crack / cocaine.
· 16 families where parent/s deemed by social worker to be using alcohol.

sample and methods
· 95 children (from 50 families) on the local child protection register on the study day.
· Review of SSD file information about family circumstances, registration category and legal status, plus questionnaire completed by child's social worker about type of drug need and perceived severity of use.

what was studied
· The relationship between different drugs and the category under which the child was registered.
· Social workers' perceptions of the impact of different drugs on children's care.

key findings
· The families where parents used drugs had a higher rate of registration for neglect and emotional abuse than the other families.
· There was a low rate of registration for physical abuse for families using drugs, and none for sexual abuse.
· Social workers deemed all but one of the families using heroin, and the one using crack/cocaine, as giving them serious cause for concern.

B10

Powis, Gossop, Bury, Payne & Griffiths

2000, Inner London

drug/s

· Most were chronic and dependant polydrug users.

· 86% used high levels of heroin in month before interview and had been using for an average of 12 years, half by injecting and half by smoking.

· Just over 50% were on methadone, a third using illicit supplies.

· Most partners also used heroin / methadone.

sample and methods

· 66 mothers who had used heroin/methadone for at least 1 year and were using at least 4 days per week at time of study.

· All had at least 1 school-age child in their care.

· 91% white, 3% mixed race, 2% black, 5% other ethnicity.

· Recruited via treatment centres and word of mouth.

· One-hour structured interview.

· Scales completed on severity of drug dependence and on mother's psychological health.

what was studied

· The profile of women drug users with children.

· Their pattern of drug (and alcohol) use.

· Their social and economic circumstances, criminal involvement and health problems.

key findings

· There was a high degree of social stress, criminal activity and mental health problems amongst the women.

· There was considerable conflict with partners.

· Mothers wanted help for their children but feared that contact with services would lead to the loss of their children.

· Parents tried hard to protect their children from the negative impact of their own or their partner's drug use.

B11

Mahoney & MacKechnie

2001, Liverpool

drug/s

· 19 of the 25 parents used drugs other than alcohol.

· Most used more than 1 drug, including heroin, methadone, stimulants and cannabis.

sample and methods

· 25 parents using drugs (or alcohol) and 20 of their children, aged 5 – 18 years.

· Just over half the parents were women.

· Half were lone parents.

· All parents but one were white.

· Just over half had at least 1 child living with them. Other children were looked after by the local authority – with relatives, other foster carers or in residential care.

· Workshop discussions about the wants and needs of a 'typical' drug-using family that participants created.

· Separate workshops for parents and children.

· 5 young people were interviewed instead of attending a workshop.

· Workshop transcripts were analysed to identify common themes.

what was studied

· The views of drug-using parents and their children about their life experiences and their use of services, in order to inform service planning by statutory and voluntary agencies.

key findings

· Although discussing a hypothetical family, respondents often talked as if relating their own experience.

· There was close agreement across the workshops and between parents and children.

· Parents knew they were failing their children and children were clear about how they were affected.

· Both children and adults saw recovery from drugs as the best outcome to hope and work for.

· The impact on children was across all areas of life – home, school, friendships and plans for the future.

B12

McKeganey, Barnard & McIntosh

2002, Scotland

drug/s

· Mainly heroin.

· Parents had used drugs for an average of 9 years.

· They had been drug free for an average of 4 years.

sample and methods

· 30 former drug users who were parents.

· Equal numbers of mothers and fathers.

· The group is a sub-group of a qualitative study of 70 adults who have recovered from heroin dependence.

· A loosely-structured interview of about 2 hours.

what was studied

Sub-sample of parents

· The impact of drug use on their children and the service implications of the findings.

Main study

· How recovery had come about, the influences that led to recovery, the challenges faced in coming off drugs, the strategies used to remain drug free, and any help received from drug treatment services.

key findings

· Parents were acutely aware of the adverse impact of drugs on their children and felt guilty and ashamed about this.

· Their drug use had affected all aspects of their children's life.

· Family circumstances had improved dramatically since parents had stopped using drugs.

B13
Kearney & Taylor
2001, Bolton, N.W.England
drug/s
· Heroin the main primary drug used.
· Methadone, amphetamine and heroin plus crack cocaine or methadone accounted for primary drug used by next largest group.
sample and methods
· 27 parents using drugs, 1 partner of a parent, and 5 grandparent carers.
· 120 qualitative interviews with parents, carers and children.
· A focus group of 8 mothers.
· 12 focus group interviews with professionals whose work included that with drug-using families (report not yet published).
what was studied
· The impact of drug use on families' daily lives and lifestyle.
· Families' views and experiences about needs and services.
key findings
· Disruption, tension and family separation were fairly high, and generally related to drug use.
· Parents acknowledged the difficulties of trying to keep to home and school routines for their children.
· The ideal service wanted by parents was practical help offered from one base and delivered in a welcoming and non-judgemental manner.
· Parents using drugs valued the support of relatives and friends.
· The service wanted by grandparent carers included continuing help for treatment after emergency placement and help for the children's emotional and behavioural problems, including the impact of loss and other trauma.

B14 (USA)
Aktan, Kumpfer & Turner
1996, USA (Detroit, Michigan)
drug/s
Not specified
sample and methods
· 88 African-American families with 1 parent in a residential drug treatment programme.
· Their children aged 6-12 years.
· Family skills training programme over 12 weeks, with sessions for parents, for children, and parents and children together.
· Evaluation interviews with participants, standardised tests of behaviour and relationships.
· Follow up at 6 and 12 months.
· Control group – included as part of the 88 families. Matching not specified.
what was studied
· Whether parents learnt to cope with children's problem behaviour and to use praise and sanctions.
· Whether children learnt to cope with loneliness, anger and peer pressure.
· Whether the programme succeeded in being culturally specific, for African-American families, as judged by families and trainers.
key findings
· Parenting efficacy increased and depression and drug use decreased.
· As rated by parents, children's aggression, depression, hyperactivity and school problems decreased.
· Time spent in parent-child activities increased.
· Family cohesion increased.
· The programme kept families involved throughout the full 12 weeks and was particularly successful in recruiting drug-using fathers.

B15 (USA)
Catalano, Gainey, Fleming, Haggerty & Johnson
1999, USA (Seattle, Washington)
drug/s
· Parents had been on methadone for at least 3 months.
sample and methods
· 144 parents (130 families) receiving treatment at 2 methadone clinics.
· And their 178 children aged 3–14 years.
· Parents mainly white, with 25 African-American and 7 'other'.
· 33 sessions of family training over 9 months, plus weekly home visit and phone contact.
· Parents and children tested at start and end of programme plus 6 and 12 months later.
· Control group – families where parents received normal methadone treatment only.
what was studied
· Any reduction in parental drug use and likely reduction by children.
· For parents – relapse, problem-solving skills, family management, peer network, domestic conflict.
· For children – adherence to rules, family attachment, parental involvement, school attendance and performance, peer network, delinquency.
key findings
· After 12 months follow up there was a significant positive change in parents' skills in parenting, family management, domestic conflict and drug use.
· Fewer changes were noted in children's behaviour or attitude.
· The more positive outcomes for children were noted for the younger children.
· The researchers suggest that the older children were resistant to parents wishing to impose new rules and boundaries on them – there were no separate training sessions for the children.

B16 (USA)
McCartt Hess, McGowan & Botsko
2000, USA (Brooklyn, New York)

drug/s
· 13% of families using the project had substance misuse problems that needed treatment.
· A range of drugs, including alcohol, but mainly crack cocaine.

sample and methods
· 301 caregivers and their 423 children (189 families) selected from the 4,630 families using the project during 2 years.
· The sample families were selected to reflect the different sizes of families and the range of difficulties.
· 3 year study, tracking progress of families through examination of case files and interviews with carers.

what was studied
· The services received by sample families and the changes in families as identified through standardised instruments.

key findings
· All but 5 children remained with their family in the neighbourhood, with the families continuing to receive help from the project.
· The researchers found that 88% of families received services to address their needs.
· Key factors identified in the programme included a family focus and orientation, the development of a client-centred relationship between family members and workers, flexibility to develop an individualised service plan for each family, easy access to staff (24 hours per day), and services continuing for as long as needed.
(note – findings relate to all families, not just those using drugs)

B17 (USA)
Shulman, Shapira & Hirshfield
2000, USA (Bronx, New York)

drug/s
· Methadone treatment

sample and methods
· 100 children of parents attending an outpatient treatment clinic.
· 61% of families were Puerto Rican.
· Children were assessed at the weekly outreach clinic.

what was studied
· Whether a multi-disciplinary team approach could encourage parents to bring children to their drug treatment clinic for health and other services.
· Child development – language, intelligence, emotional and behavioural and other disorders.
· Child health – feeding, asthma, heart function, obesity, failure to thrive.

key findings
· A high proportion of the children had special needs, especially speech and/or language impairment and medical and/or nutritional disorders.
· 72% of the children assessed and then referred on to specialist services were receiving the recommended services at follow up. This compares favourably with the team's previous practice of referring children to another site much earlier – fewer than 10 % of children were able to be assessed, let alone referred for services.
· The flexible and accessible children's services provided by the team encouraged greater participation by parents.

B18 (USA)
Moore & Finkelstein
2001, USA (Massachusetts)

drug/s
· Not specified, but includes alcohol too.

sample and methods
· Parenting training piloted in the community and later delivered in 11 residential treatment centres.
· 18 sessions, each of 90 minutes, covering parenting training, adult development, family relationships and cultural heritage.
· 170 women started the programmes, just over a third completed the final evaluation.
· Evaluation by standard measurements (at admission & completion) and participants' comments.

what was studied
· Whether parenting competence and confidence improved.
· Whether drug treatment workers could increase their ability to respond to parent-child, child welfare and family issues.

key findings
· For those who completed the programme there were significant improvements in self-esteem and in parenting knowledge and attitudes.
· Parents showed significant improvements in empathising with children's needs and in not expecting children to act as young carers. Less progress was made in having reasonable expectations of what children could do and achieve, and in reducing belief in the efficiency of corporal punishment.
· The programme helped nurture more trusting and collaborative relationships between substance abuse and child welfare systems.
· Participants rated the programme highly in terms of strengthening family relationships and strengthening their own recovery.

B19
Kearney & Ibbetson
1991, Inner London
drug/s
· Methadone.
· Almost half of their partners used heroin or methadone at the time of study.
sample and methods
· The 12 pregnant women from one local authority who used the hospital's antenatal clinic in the study period.
· Review of social work records and medical notes and follow-up for up to 3 years by review of file material and discussion with professionals involved with the family.
what was studied
Whether the contribution of one social worker in the hospital's obstetric team and another in the adult psychiatric service (drugs) increased the chances of engaging with mothers using drugs.
key findings
· Hospital and community social care professionals succeeded in maintaining good contact with mothers after discharge, even though mothers were in temporary accommodation and some moved out of the catchment area.
· The joint planning arrangements succeeded in offering parents help with their drug problem and other needs, even if there was no child protection action.
· An identified risk factor was the mothers' previous lack of success in parenting a child.
· Identified protective factors included suitable permanent housing and support from the extended family, especially grandparents.

B20
Keen, Oliver, Rowse & Mathers
2000, Sheffield
drug/s
· Mainly heroin plus other drugs.
· Mainly injecting.
· 10 on methadone prior to admission.
sample and methods
· 26 parents and their 33 children (23 families) who entered a residential, family-based drug treatment service in the study year.
· 4 of the parents were fathers.
· 22 parents were white, 4 black, none Asian.
· A retrospective analysis of the clinical and other file records kept at the centre.
what was studied
· For parents – their length of stay and reason for departure.
· For children – reason for departure and whether they returned home with parent/s.
key findings
· A third of the adults completed treatment successfully. This is comparable to results from residential settings without children, suggesting that a family setting can be used for both detox and rehabilitation.
· Older parents, and those not polydrug users, had significantly better outcomes than others.
· Little information was found on files about the children.
· The good progress made by some parents meant that children not living with them at the start of the treatment were able to return to their care.

B21
Harbin
2002, Bolton, N.W.England
drug/s
· Heroin the predominant drug.
· Some parents on methadone.
· Most were polydrug users.
· In 4 of the 5 two-parent families both parents used drugs.
sample and methods
· A 6 month pilot project, for 8 families (14 children aged new-born to 13 years).
· All families had a multi-agency action plan in place because of concerns about the significantly detrimental effects of parental drug use on the children.
· Project offered an intensive, one-stop shop for families.
· Services included priority referrals to other local resources, individual appointments, drop-in sessions and children's groups, plus 3 outreach workers for work in family home outside office hours.
· Project based in community family centre.
what was studied
· Whether the project enabled children to be free from significant harm (or risk of it) with their parents.
key findings
· Parents benefited from receiving services from a local, accessible, child-friendly base.
· All but one child remained living safely with parents.
· It was possible to provide some universal and specialist support services from the project's base (health visiting, midwifery, drugs' team).
· Staff gained from the experience of working closely with colleagues from other agencies.
· The families remained involved in the Centre after the project ended.
· The family support outreach work was not as costly as had been anticipated and was highly regarded by parents and children.

B22

Hayden, Jerrim & Pike
2002, Portsmouth

drug/s

· Cannabis, heroin, methadone, polydrug use.

sample and methods

· Pilot project, offering link worker to 59 families over 9 month period, referred by social workers and other agencies.

what was studied

· Nature of work of link worker.
· Services received by families after referral.
· Views of parents about their need for support and evaluation of support received.

key findings

· The most commonly used substance was cannabis or heroin, but referring social workers thought it was alcohol.
· 90% of parents felt it important to stop using, but only 40% felt some confidence about succeeding.
· All the parents wanted support for their children.
· Disadvantages of residential services included disruption to children's schooling, lack of child care, time needed away from home.

references

A   research and literature reviews

A1

Hogan, D. M. (1998) Annotation: The Psychological Development and Welfare of Children of Opiate and Cocaine Users: Review and Research Needs. *Journal of Child Psychology and Psychiatry*, 39 (5) 609-620. This is a review of USA studies.

A2

Keen, J. and Alison, L.H. (2001) Drug misusing parents: key points for health professionals. *Archives of Disease in Childhood*, 85, 296-299. This is a review of British and international studies, with a focus on health issues.

A3

Hayden, C., Jerrim, S. and Pike, S. (2002) *Parental Substance Misuse - the impact on child care social work caseloads.* Report No. 47. Social Services Research and Information Unit (SSRIU), University of Portsmouth. This includes a review of British and international studies, including alcohol as well as drugs, and with information about national and local prevalence.

A4

Barnard, M. (2001) *Intervening with drug dependent parents and their children: what is the problem and what is being done to help?* Centre for Drug Misuse Research, University of Glasgow. This includes a review of British and international studies.

B   single studies

B1

Burns, E., O'Driscoll, M. and Wason, G. (1996) The Health and Development of Children whose Mothers are on Methadone Maintenance. *Child Abuse Review*, 5, 113-122.

B2

Alison, L. and Wyatt, S. (1998) *A Study to Determine whether Maternal Substance Misuse in Pregnancy in Sheffield is a Risk Factor for Child Abuse and Neglect.* Department of Paediatrics, University of Leeds and The Children's Hospital, Sheffield.

B3

Jayasooriya, S. (2000) *The nature and location of primary care services received by the children of people with intravenous substance misuse problems registered at The Primary Care Unit.* Unpublished research report, University of London.

B4

Hogan, D. and Higgins, L. (2001) *When Parents Use Drugs – Key Findings from a Study of Children in the Care of Drug-using Parents.* The Children's Research Centre, Trinity College, Dublin.

B5

Powell, J. (1995) *Drug Use and Parenting.* Unpublished dissertation. London School of Economics and Kings College, London.

B6

Klee, H. and Jackson, M. (1998) *Illicit Drug Use, Pregnancy and Early Motherhood. Report to the Department of Health Task Force to Review Services for Drug Misusers.* Centre for Social Research on Health and Substance Abuse (SRHSA), Manchester Metropolitan University.

B7

Centre for Social Research on Health and Substance Abuse (SRHSA) (1998) *Drug Using Parents and their Children - Risk and Protective Factors. A Preliminary Study. Final Report to the Department of Health.* SRHSA, Manchester Metropolitan University.

B8

Elliott, E. and Watson, A. (1998) *Fit to be a Parent. The needs of drug using parents in Salford and Trafford.* Research Report 8. Public Health Research and Resource Centre (PHRRC), University of Salford.

B9

Forrester, D. (2000) Parental Substance Misuse and Child Protection in a British Sample, *Child Abuse Review,* 9, 235-246.

B10

Powis, B., Gossop, M., Bury, C., Payne, K. and Griffiths, P. (2000) Drug-using mothers: social, psychological and substance use problems of women opiate users with children. *Drug and Alcohol Review,* 19, 171-180.

B11

Mahoney, C. and MacKechnie, S. (2001) *In a Different World. Parental drug and alcohol use: a consultation into its effects on children and families in Liverpool.* Liverpool Health Authority.

B12

McKeganey, N., Barnard, M. and McIntosh, J. (2002) Paying the Price for their Parents' Drug Use: The Impact of Parental Drug Use on Children. *Drug Education, Prevention and Policy,* 3, 233-246. The study of all 70 recovered heroin users, rather than the 30 who were parents, is McIntosh, J. and McKeganey, N. (2002) *Beating the Dragon: The Recovery from Dependent Drug Use.* Prentice Hall.

B13
Kearney, J. and Taylor, N. (2001) *The Highs and Lows of Family Life. Report of a two-year research project.* Bolton Home-Start/Institute for Public Health Research and Policy (IPHRP), University of Salford.

B14
Aktan, G.B., Kumpfer, K. and Turner, C.W. (1996) Effectiveness of a Family Skills Training Program for Substance Use Prevention with Inner City African-American Families. *Substance Use & Misuse*, 31 (2) 157-175. For details about how the programme was developed, see Aktan, G.B. (1998) Evolution of a Substance Abuse Prevention Program with Inner City African-American Families. *Drugs & Society*, (The Haworth Press, Inc.) 12 (1/2) 39-52.

B15
Catalano, R.F., Gainey, R.R., Fleming, C.B., Haggerty, K.P. and Johnson, N.O. (1999) An experimental intervention with families of substance abusers: one-year follow-up of the focus on families project. *Addiction*, 94 (2) 241-254.

B16
McCartt Hess, P., McGowan, B.G. and Botsko, M. (2000) A Preventive Services Program Model for Preserving and Supporting Families Over Time. *Child Welfare League of America*, 79 (3) 227-265.

B17
Shulman, L.H., Shapira, M.A. and Hirshfield, M.A. (2000) Outreach Developmental Services to Children of Patients in Treatment for Substance Abuse. *American Journal of Public Health*, 90 (12) 1930-1933.

B18
Moore, J. and Finkelstein, N. (2001) Parenting Services for Families Affected by Substance Abuse. *Child Welfare League of America*, 80 (2) 221-238.

B19
Kearney, P. and Ibbetson, M. (1991) Opiate Dependent Women and Their Babies: A Study of the Multi-disciplinary Work of a Hospital and a Local Authority. *British Journal of Social Work*, 21 (2) 105-126.

B20
Keen, J., Oliver, P., Rowse, G. and Mathers, N. (2000) Keeping families of heroin addicts together: results of 13 months' intake for community detoxification and rehabilitation at a family centre for drug users. *Family Practice*, 17 (6) 484-489.

B21
Harbin, F. (2002) *The Safer Families Project*. Report for Bolton ACPC.

B22
Hayden, C., Jerrim, S. and Pike, S. (2002) Section 6: Research Findings - a pilot project. In A3.

C   practice and policy documents

C1
Department of Health, Department for Education and Employment, Home Office (2000). *Framework for the Assessment of Children in Need and their Families*. The Stationery Office.

C2
Tunnard, J. (2002) *Parental problem drinking and its impact on children*. **research** in **practice**.

C3
Scottish Executive (2001) *Getting our priorities right: policy and practice guidelines for working with children and families affected by problem drug use. A consultation paper*. The Stationery Office.

C4
DrugScope (2000) *UK Drug Situation 2000 - The UK report to the European Monitoring Centre for Drugs and Drug Addiction (EMCDDA)*. DrugScope.

C5
Singleton, N., Bumpstead, R., O'Brien, M., Lee, A. and Meltzer, H. (2000) *Psychiatric Morbidity Among Adults living in Private Households*. Office for National Statistics.

C6
Cleaver, H., Unell, I. and Aldgate, J. (1999) *Children's Needs - Parenting Capacity. The impact of parental mental illness, problem alcohol and drug use, and domestic violence on children's development*. The Stationery Office.

C7
Tunnard, J. (2002) Matching Needs and Services: Emerging Themes from its Application in Different Social Care Settings. In Ward, H. and Rose, W. (eds) *Approaches to Needs Assessment in Children's Services*. Jessica Kingsley.

C8
HM Government (1998) *Tackling Drugs to build a Better Britain*. This functions as the UK and English Strategy. Scotland and Northern Ireland published a similar document in 1999, and Wales in 2000 (but including alcohol).

C9
National Treatment Outcome Research Study. For information about NTORS and project development contact the website: www.ntors.org.uk

C10
Harbin, F. and Murphy, M. (eds) (2000) *Substance Misuse and Child Care - How to Understand, Assist and Intervene when Drugs Affect Parenting.* Russell House.

C11
Hayes, G. (ed.) (2002) *Drugnotes 1-10,* (including 1- Heroin, 4 - Amphetamines, 5 - Cocaine & crack). DrugScope.

C12
Famularo, R., Kinscherff, R. and Fenton, T. (1992) Parental substance abuse and the nature of child maltreatment. *Child Abuse and Neglect,* 16, 475-483.

C13
Dearden, S., Aldridge, J. and Dearden, S. (1998) *Young Carers and their Families.* Blackwell Science.

C14
Keen, J., Rowse, G., Mathers, N., Campbell, M. and Seivewright, N. (2000) Can methadone maintenance for heroin-dependent patients retained in general practice reduce criminal conviction rates and time spent in prison? *British Journal of General Practice,* 50, 48-49.

C15
SCODA (1997) *Drug Using Parents: Policy Guidelines for Inter-agency working.* LGA Publications.

C16
Harwin, J., Owen, M., Locke, M. and Forrester, D. (forthcoming) *Making Care Orders Work: A Study of Care Plans and their Implementation.* The Stationery Office.

C17
Dartington Social Research Unit (2001) *Matching Needs and Services* (3rd ed.). A Dartington-i practice tool. Dartington Academic Press.

C18
Dillon, K. (2001) *Children's Services Plan, 2001-2002.* And *Children and Families Service: Parental Substance Misuse Project.* Project Outline. London Borough of Sutton.

C19
Powell, J. and Hart, D. (2001) Working with Parents who Use Drugs, in *FRAGILE: Handle with Care (a training pack),* NSPCC.

C20
Murphy, M. and Harbin, F. (2000) Background and Current Context of Substance Misuse and Child Care. In C10 (above).

C21
Rutter, M. (1990) Psychosocial resilience and protective mechanisms.
In Rolf, J., Masten, A.S., Cichetti, D., Nuechterlin, K.H. and
Weintraub, S. (eds) *Risk and protective factors in the development of
psychopathology*. Cambridge University Press.

C22
Pearce, J. and Holmes, S.P. (1994) *Health Gain Investment Programme.
Technical Review Document. People with Mental Health Problems (part four)
Child and Adolescent Mental Health*. NHS Executive Trent and Centre for
Mental Health Service Development.

C23
Department of Health (2002) *Dual Diagnosis Provision*. Department of
Health.

C24
Merton College (2002) *Being a Parent* - a course developed by the
Drugs Action Team in the London Borough of Merton, the Parenting
Unit at Merton College, Surrey, and local specialist drug agencies.

C25
Butt, J. and Box, L. (1998) *Family Centred. A study of the use of family
centres by black families*. REU.

C26
Race Equality Unit (2001) Strengthening Families, Issue 1, *The
newsletter of Strengthening Families, Strengthening Communities*, REU.

C27
Henggeler, S.W. and Borduin, C.M. (1990) *Family Therapy and Beyond:
A Multi-Systemic Approach to Treating the Behaviour Problems of Children and
Adolescents*. Brooks/Cole.

C28
Morris, K., Marsh, P. and Wiffen, J. (1998) *Family Group Conferences: A
Training Pack*. The Family Rights Group.

C29
Ryan, M. (2000) *Working with Fathers*. Radcliffe Medical Press.

C30
Jacobs, J. (1998) *The links between substance misuse and domestic violence -
current knowledge and debates*. Alcohol Concern and the Institute for the
Study of Drug Dependence.

C31
Copello, A., Orford, J., Velleman, R., Templeton, L. and Krishnan, M.
(2000) Methods for reducing alcohol and drug related family harm in
non-specialist settings. *Journal of Mental Health*, 9, 329-343.

C32
Meyers, R. J., Miller, W. R., Hill, D. E., and Tonigan, R. S. (1999)
Community reinforcement and family training (CRAFT): Engaging
unmotivated drug users in treatment. *Journal of Substance Abuse*, 10 (3)
1-18. Cited in DrugScope (2000) *Drug and Alcohol Findings*, Issue 4.

C33
The Queen on the Application of L and Others v Manchester City
Council. The Queen on the Application of R and Another v
Manchester City Council. Reported in January (2002) *Family Law*.

C34
Patel, K. (2000) The Missing Drug Users: Minority ethnic drug users
and their children. In C10 (above).

C35
Kmietowicz, Z. (2002) GPs asked to do more for drug misusers.
British Medical Journal, 324, 2 March, 501. Reporting on *Changing
Habits: The Commissioning and Management of Community Drug Treatment
Services for Adults*, available at www.audit-commission.gov.uk

C36
Reder, P. and Lucey, C. (eds) (1995) *Assessment of parenting: psychiatric
and psychological contributions*. Routledge.

C37
Kelly, L. and Humphreys, C. (2000) *Reducing Domestic Violence... What
Works? Outreach and Advocacy Approaches*. Policing and Reducing Crime
Briefing Note, Home Office.

C38
Gilligan, R. (1998) The importance of schools and teachers in child
welfare. *Child and Family Social Work*. 3, 13-25.

C39
Sykes, D.H., Hoy, E.A., Bill, J.M., McClure, B.G., Halliday, H.L. and
Reid, M.M. (1997) Behavioural Adjustment in School of Very Low
Birthweight Children. *Journal of Child Psychology and Psychiatry*, 38, (3)
315-325.

references listed alphabetically, by author

The code at the end of each reference refers to the place in the list above.

Alison, L. and Wyatt, S. (1998) *A Study to Determine whether Maternal Substance Misuse in Pregnancy in Sheffield is a Risk Factor for Child Abuse and Neglect.* Department of Paediatrics, University of Leeds and The Children's Hospital, Sheffield. B2

Aktan, G.B., Kumpfer, K. and Turner, C.W. (1996) Effectiveness of a Family Skills Training Program for Substance Use Prevention with Inner City African-American Families. *Substance Use & Misuse*, 31 (2) 157-175. For details about how the programme was developed, see Aktan, G.B. (1998) Evolution of a Substance Abuse Prevention Program with Inner City African-American Families. *Drugs & Society*, (The Haworth Press, Inc.) 12 (1/2) 39-52. B14

Barnard, M. (2001) *Intervening with drug dependent parents and their children: what is the problem and what is being done to help?* Centre for Drug Misuse Research, University of Glasgow. A4

Burns, E., O'Driscoll, M. and Wason, G. (1996) The Health and Development of Children whose Mothers are on Methadone Maintenance. *Child Abuse Review*, 5, 113-122. B1

Butt, J. and Box, L. (1998) *Family Centred. A study of the use of family centres by black families.* REU. C25

Catalano, R.F., Gainey, R.R., Fleming, C.B., Haggerty, K.P. and Johnson, N.O. (1999) An experimental intervention with families of substance abusers: one-year follow-up of the focus on families project. *Addiction*, 94 (2) 241-254. B15

Centre for Social Research on Health and Substance Abuse (SRHSA) (1998) *Drug Using Parents and their Children - Risk and Protective Factors. A Preliminary Study. Final Report to the Department of Health.* SRHSA, Manchester Metropolitan University. B7

Cleaver, H., Unell, I. and Aldgate, J. (1999) *Children's Needs - Parenting Capacity. The impact of parental mental illness, problem alcohol and drug use, and domestic violence on children's development.* The Stationery Office. C6

Copello, A., Orford, J., Velleman, R., Templeton, L. and Krishnan, M. (2000) Methods for reducing alcohol and drug related family harm in non-specialist settings. *Journal of Mental Health*, 9, 329-343. C31

Dartington Social Research Unit (2001) *Matching Needs and Services* (3rd ed.). A Dartington-i practice tool. Dartington Academic Press. C17

Dearden, S., Aldridge, J. and Dearden, S. (1998) *Young Carers and their Families.* Blackwell Science. C13

Department of Health (2002) *Dual Diagnosis Provision*. Department of Health. C23

Department of Health, Department for Education and Employment, Home Office (2000). *Framework for the Assessment of Children in Need and their Families*. The Stationery Office. C1

Dillon, K. (2001) *Children's Services Plan, 2001-2002. And Children and Families Service: Parental Substance Misuse Project. Project Outline*. London Borough of Sutton. C18

DrugScope (2000) *UK Drug Situation 2000 - The UK report to the European Monitoring Centre for Drugs and Drug Addiction (EMCDDA)*. DrugScope. C4

Elliott, E. and Watson, A. (1998) *Fit to be a Parent. The needs of drug using parents in Salford and Trafford*. Research Report 8. Public Health Research and Resource Centre (PHRRC), University of Salford. B8

Famularo, R., Kinscherff, R. and Fenton, T. (1992) Parental substance abuse and the nature of child maltreatment. *Child Abuse and Neglect*, 16, 475-483. C12

Forrester, D. (2000) Parental Substance Misuse and Child Protection in a British Sample, *Child Abuse Review*, 9, 235-246. B9

Gilligan, R. (1998) The importance of schools and teachers in child welfare. *Child and Family Social Work*. 3, 13-25. C38

Harbin, F. (2002) *The Safer Families Project*. Report for Bolton ACPC. B21

Harbin, F. and Murphy, M. (eds) (2000) *Substance Misuse and Child Care - How to Understand, Assist and Intervene when Drugs Affect Parenting*. Russell House. C10

Harwin, J., Owen, M., Locke, M. and Forrester, D. (forthcoming) *Making Care Orders Work: A Study of Care Plans and their Implementation*. The Stationery Office. C16

Hayden, C., Jerrim, S. and Pike, S. (2002) *Parental Substance Misuse - the impact on child care social work caseloads*. Report No. 47. Social Services Research and Information Unit (SSRIU), University of Portsmouth. A3 and B22

Hayes, G. (ed.) (2002) *Drugnotes 1-10*, (including 1- Heroin, 4 - Amphetamines, 5 - Cocaine & crack). DrugScope. C11

Henggeler, S.W. and Borduin, C.M. (1990) *Family Therapy and Beyond: A Multi-Systemic Approach to Treating the Behaviour Problems of Children and Adolescents*. Brooks/Cole. C27

HM Government (1998) *Tackling Drugs to build a Better Britain*. This functions as the UK and English Strategy. Scotland and Northern Ireland published a similar document in 1999, and Wales in 2000 (but including alcohol). C8

Hogan, D. M. (1998) Annotation: The Psychological Development and Welfare of Children of Opiate and Cocaine Users: Review and Research Needs. *Journal of Child Psychology and Psychiatry*, 39 (5) 609-620. A1

Hogan, D. and Higgins, L. (2001) *When Parents Use Drugs – Key Findings from a Study of Children in the Care of Drug-using Parents*. The Children's Research Centre, Trinity College, Dublin. B4

Jacobs, J. (1998) *The links between substance misuse and domestic violence - current knowledge and debates*. Alcohol Concern and the Institute for the Study of Drug Dependence. C30

Jayasooriya, S. (2000) *The nature and location of primary care services received by the children of people with intravenous substance misuse problems registered at The Primary Care Unit*. Unpublished research report, University of London. B3

Kearney, P. and Ibbetson, M. (1991) Opiate Dependent Women and Their Babies: A Study of the Multi-disciplinary Work of a Hospital and a Local Authority. *British Journal of Social Work*, 21 (2) 105-126. B19

Kearney, J. and Taylor, N. (2001) *The Highs and Lows of Family Life. Report of a two-year research project*. Bolton Home-Start/Institute for Public Health Research and Policy (IPHRP), University of Salford. B13

Keen, J. and Alison, L.H. (2001) Drug misusing parents: key points for health professionals. *Archives of Disease in Childhood*, 85, 296-299. A2

Keen, J., Oliver, P., Rowse, G. and Mathers, N. (2000) Keeping families of heroin addicts together: results of 13 months' intake for community detoxification and rehabilitation at a family centre for drug users. *Family Practice*, 17 (6) 484-489. B20

Keen, J., Rowse, G., Mathers, N., Campbell, M. and Seivewright, N. (2000) Can methadone maintenance for heroin-dependent patients retained in general practice reduce criminal conviction rates and time spent in prison? *British Journal of General Practice*, 50, 48-49. C14

Kelly, L. and Humphreys, C. (2000) *Reducing Domestic Violence... What Works? Outreach and Advocacy Approaches*. Policing and Reducing Crime Briefing Note, Home Office. C37

Klee, H. and Jackson, M. (1998) *Illicit Drug Use, Pregnancy and Early Motherhood. Report to the Department of Health Task Force to Review Services for Drug Misusers.* Centre for Social Research on Health and Substance Abuse (SRHSA), Manchester Metropolitan University. B6

Kmietowicz, Z. (2002) GPs asked to do more for drug misusers. *British Medical Journal,* 324, 2 March, 501. Reporting on *Changing Habits: The Commissioning and Management of Community Drug Treatment Services for Adults,* available at www.audit-commission.gov.uk C35

Mahoney, C. and MacKechnie, S. (2001) *In a Different World. Parental drug and alcohol use: a consultation into its effects on children and families in Liverpool.* Liverpool Health Authority. B11

McCartt Hess, P., McGowan, B.G. and Botsko, M. (2000) A Preventive Services Program Model for Preserving and Supporting Families Over Time. *Child Welfare League of America,* 79 (3) 227-265. B16

McKeganey, N., Barnard, M. and McIntosh, J. (2002) Paying the Price for their Parents' Drug Use: The Impact of Parental Drug Use on Children. *Drug Education, Prevention and Policy,* 3, 233-246. The study of all 70 recovered heroin users, rather than the 30 who were parents, is McIntosh, J. and McKeganey, N. (2002) *Beating the Dragon: The Recovery from Dependent Drug Use.* Prentice Hall. B12

Merton College (2002) *Being a Parent* - a course developed by the Drugs Action Team in the London Borough of Merton, the Parenting Unit at Merton College, Surrey, and local specialist drug agencies. C24

Meyers, R. J., Miller, W. R., Hill, D. E., and Tonigan, R. S. (1999) Community reinforcement and family training (CRAFT): Engaging unmotivated drug users in treatment. *Journal of Substance Abuse,* 10 (3) 1-18. Cited in DrugScope (2000) *Drug and Alcohol Findings,* Issue 4. C32

Moore, J. and Finkelstein, N. (2001) Parenting Services for Families Affected by Substance Abuse. *Child Welfare League of America,* 80 (2) 221-238. B18

Morris, K., Marsh, P. and Wiffen, J. (1998) *Family Group Conferences: A Training Pack.* The Family Rights Group. C28

Murphy, M. and Harbin, F. (2000) Background and Current Context of Substance Misuse and Child Care. In C10 (above). C20

National Treatment Outcome Research Study. For information about NTORS and project development contact the website: www.ntors.org.uk C9

Patel, K. (2000) The Missing Drug Users: Minority ethnic drug users and their children. In C10 (above). C34

Pearce, J. and Holmes, S.P. (1994) *Health Gain Investment Programme. Technical Review Document. People with Mental Health Problems (part four) Child and Adolescent Mental Health.* NHS Executive Trent and Centre for Mental Health Service Development. C22

Powell, J. (1995) *Drug Use and Parenting.* Unpublished dissertation. London School of Economics and Kings College, London. B5

Powell, J. and Hart, D. (2001) Working with Parents who Use Drugs, in FRAGILE: *Handle with Care (a training pack),* NSPCC. C19

Powis, B., Gossop, M., Bury, C., Payne, K. and Griffiths, P. (2000) Drug-using mothers: social, psychological and substance use problems of women opiate users with children. *Drug and Alcohol Review,* 19, 171-180. B10

Race Equality Unit (2001) Strengthening Families, Issue 1, *The newsletter of Strengthening Families, Strengthening Communities,* REU. C26

Reder, P. and Lucey, C. (eds) (1995) *Assessment of parenting: psychiatric and psychological contributions.* Routledge. C36

Rutter, M. (1990) Psychosocial resilience and protective mechanisms. In Rolf, J., Masten, A.S., Cichetti, D., Nuechterlin, K.H. and Weintraub, S. (eds) *Risk and protective factors in the development of psychopathology.* Cambridge University Press. C21

Ryan, M. (2000) *Working with Fathers.* Radcliffe Medical Press. C29

SCODA (1997) *Drug Using Parents: Policy Guidelines for Inter-agency working.* LGA Publications. C15

Scottish Executive (2001) *Getting our priorities right: policy and practice guidelines for working with children and families affected by problem drug use. A consultation paper.* The Stationery Office. C3

Shulman, L.H., Shapira, M.A. and Hirshfield, M.A. (2000) Outreach Developmental Services to Children of Patients in Treatment for Substance Abuse. *American Journal of Public Health,* 90 (12) 1930-1933. B17

Singleton, N., Bumpstead, R., O'Brien, M., Lee, A. and Meltzer, H. (2000) *Psychiatric Morbidity Among Adults living in Private Households.* Office for National Statistics. C5

Sykes, D.H., Hoy, E.A., Bill, J.M., McClure, B.G., Halliday, H.L. and Reid, M.M. (1997) Behavioural Adjustment in School of Very Low Birthweight Children. *Journal of Child Psychology and Psychiatry,* 38 (3) 315-325. C39

The Queen on the Application of L and Others v Manchester City Council. The Queen on the Application of R and Another v Manchester City Council. Reported in January (2002) *Family Law.* C33

Tunnard, J. (2002) *Parental problem drinking and its impact on children.* **research** in **practice.** C2

Tunnard, J. (2002) Matching Needs and Services: Emerging Themes from its Application in Different Social Care Settings. In Ward, H. and Rose, W. (eds) *Approaches to Needs Assessment in Children's Services.* Jessica Kingsley. C7 about the author

Jo Tunnard works as an independent researcher, writer and editor
for a range of statutory and non-governmental organisations,
including both adult and children's divisions of the Department of
Health. She also has twenty years' experience of working in NGOs
concerned with advising families about their rights to welfare
benefits and enabling families to have a voice in decisions made by
social services departments and the courts about their children and
young relatives. She is a founder member of RTB Associates:
www.ryantunnardbrown.com.